Mountain Mists:
Appalachian Folkways of West Virginia

Dr. Carol Ann Gillespie

McClain Printing Company
Parsons, WV
www.mcclainprinting.com
2009

International Standard Book Number 0-87012-790-X
Library of Congress Control Number 2009907418
Printed in the United States of America
Copyright © 2009 by Dr. Carol Ann Gillespie
Cranberry Township, PA
All Rights Reserved
2009

Preface

Mountain Mists: Appalachian Folkways of West Virginia is a book about some of the Appalachian folkways of the people of West Virginia. A few of the topics included in this book are traditional foods, folk remedies to cure sickness, customs associated with death and dying, as well as the importance of premonitions and tokens in early settlers' lives.

The majority of original settlers to this region were from Germany, England, Scotland, and Ireland. They were farmers who moved to these fertile mountains and coves to buy land at low cost and escape the tyranny of rich land owners in the old country. The fertile soils and lush forests welcomed them as the Appalachian Mountains, even back then, were an ancient mountain chain with deeply-cut streams and rivers and rounded mountaintops. While material possessions were few, these original West Virginians brought a vast knowledge of the traditional ways of life. Many of their foods, healing remedies and cures, and farming know-how came from the old country. However, as they adapted to the mountains, they synthesized these old ways with newer strategies that were a better fit for this wild and strange land. Sometimes they embraced the knowledge of indigenous Native Americans who taught them much about the fruits, roots, barks, and berries of their new mountain home. While they adhered faithfully to their largely Protestant Christian faith, these early settlers also steadfastly believed in the old ways of sorcery and witchcraft. This interesting dichotomy of belief systems resulted in the creation of a fascinating blend of folkways that became part of the oral tradition of the Appalachian region.

As these early mountain folk went about their daily lives, they preserved their folkways in the form of stories and songs so that later generations now have a rich reserve of these earliest settlers' lives. These stories were told around the hearth in the long winter evenings while the winds blew and snow piled high against the cabin walls. This rich oral tradition has been preserved through the years and forms an integral part of the Appalachian cultural heritage.

Today many of these folkways still form an important part of the mountaineer's life. In describing the folk customs of early West Virginians, this book tells a continuing story of the lives of the people of West Virginia. Much of what you read in these pages will tickle your memories. You may have heard a grandparent or family member tell stories that relate to these folkways. Some of these folkways continue to this day, although for how much longer – who can say? I have tried to gather in one book a small portion of the collective memory of West Virginians who are no longer with us as well as those who still recollect the old ways.

Unlike the historian who relies largely on public documents to tell the story, I have used both oral and written records to craft this book of folkways. Much of folk culture is passed down by word of mouth and therefore cannot be corroborated by experts or written records. These stories and folkways are part of the oral tradition of West Virginia's cultural heritage. Some of the information in this book has been gleaned from authoritative sources who receive ample credit for their research and work. But most of what lies within is part of the living, breathing, oral tradition of the people of West Virginia.

Also, this book is not, nor was it ever intended to be, a comprehensive or all-inclusive collection of West Virginia folk ways. Important segments of the folk culture such as music, art, architecture, and drama, for example, are not included. This is not to say they are not equally important pieces of our past. It was just not possible to cover everything in one book so I focused on topics closest to my heart. Nor can I assert that this book is the definitive authority on a topic that is covered. There is still much information out there that has not been captured or written down and may soon be lost as our rich heritage of older generations pass on. My intent was to introduce each topic and pique your interest sufficiently so that you will continue to read and seek out more information on the topic. I have tried to inform, entertain, and preserve in some small way the quilt work of West Virginia's folk culture while maintaining as much accuracy as possible.

Last, I have written this book- not for the scholars of Appalachian studies or the professors of West Virginia history – but for the average West Virginian to read and relish. This book is meant to be enjoyed on the porch with a cup of coffee in one hand. It is meant to be read on a snowy night by a crackling fire as the wind whistles down the chimney. Most importantly, it is meant to be shared with your children and grandchildren.

This is their story. This is their history. This is their roots.

About the Author:

Dr. Carol Ann Gillespie lives in Cranberry Township, Pennsylvania with her husband, Michael. They have three sons- Joshua, David, and Kevin – who were born and raised in West Virginia. Carol Ann is a frequent contributor to *Wonderful West Virginia* magazine and has written several books and articles on geography topics. As a cultural geographer, she loves the rich heritage and culture of West Virginia and spends most of her weekends and summers with her husband, Michael, exploring the mountains and talking with the people she meets on her way.

Chapter 1

Tokens, Premonitions, and Superstitions

The stories passed along by word of mouth in the oral tradition help frame the folk culture of West Virginia. The most important thing about these stories is not just what actually happened, but rather what people **believe** happened. Folk stories passed down from generation to generation constitute a shared experience that transcends the cold, hard factual existence of past lives. People are interested in and respect stories that are handed down because they are about everyday people living their daily lives. These tales become a part of our present reality. Changing slightly with each retelling, these tales captivate us and continue to send shivers up our spines to this very day.

This chapter describes the belief in tokens, premonitions, and superstitions that compose such an important part of the folk culture of West Virginia.

Tokens- Premonitions of Future Events

Appalachian folklore is full of the belief in tokens – premonitions of events to come. Tokens are also referred to as "omens." Old-timers can also be heard referring to tokens as "stage signs" or "happenings." Since the very beginning of mankind on this Earth, humans have always observed the changing of the seasons and the signs that portended these events. Perhaps the inevitability of these signs and the corresponding changes that followed prompted humans to accept omens and tokens in every area of their lives as seriously as they would religious precepts. These signs were not requested but were given anyway, and the wise knew they signified something and gave heed. Our ancestors feared the unknown and came to rely on certain "signs" or tokens as warnings of an event, especially death. Perhaps this was simply a way of trying to gain some small measure of control over one's life in a world full of unknown dangers and uncertainties.

The dictionary defines an omen as an occurrence that is regarded as a sign of how somebody or something will fare in the future. Belief in both good and bad omens, or tokens, dominated the lives of the early settlers of the Appalachian Mountains. Since the majority of these early settlers were Scotch-Irish, they were descendents of the Celts who came to the British Isles around B.C. 250. The Celtic people were a superstitious group. The knowledge they relied on for daily living came from their surroundings and the stories passed on to them generation to generation over the centuries. Hence, folk wisdom and stories were woven into the very fabric of their lives and became superstitions that accompanied them across the ocean to the Appalachian Mountains.

Good omens were believed to be signs of coming good luck and included catching a falling leaf, dreaming of clear water, and finding a rusty nail. Omens that warned of bad luck included sneezing before breakfast, walking under a ladder, and skipping a row when planting corn. Of course, we all know the bad luck that will come if a black cat crosses our path or we break a mirror (that's good for seven years of bad luck)! But did you know that if you hear a strange ticking in a room and there is no clock around, in a very short time someone will die in that room!

In the Appalachian Mountains of West Virginia, even animals have premonitions. My father-in-law liked to tell the following story at family get-togethers. His father, William Gillespie, worked for Eureka Oil and Gas and also ran the telegraph in Macfarlan, Ritchie County. During the late 1930's, he lived in a house along the banks of Macfarlan Creek about one mile from the main highway. William started to notice that his faithful dog, Old Joe, would get up from his dreams of rabbit hunting and walk to the bus stop on the main highway whenever one of William's daughters, Virginia or Vernita, was arriving for a visit! Even William had no foreknowledge that his daughters were planning to come home. The neighbors always remarked that Bill was going to get some company when they saw Old Joe patiently waiting at the bus stop. How could this old hound dog know that a family member was coming on the bus? Old Joe never made his trek to the bus stop for any other reason or on any other occasion. Somehow the old hound had a premonition that they were coming for a visit because he never missed greeting the girls and welcoming them home!

Omens and tokens are often fear-inducing. West Virginia columnist and author, Alyce Faye Bragg, in her book *This Holler is My Home*, recalls how tokens terrified her as a child. She was so afraid she would see a token that she refused to go into the barn to get stored onions in broad daylight! She tells the story of the light that was seen the night her Granny Cottrell died. The family had gathered at Granny's home to keep a vigil as her death was rapidly approaching. As family members huddled around the kitchen stove for warmth, they noticed a beam of light, similar to a flashlight, shining on the chicken house. The light grew steadily larger and larger until it was an enormous circle covering the side of the shed. Then it started to shrink in size until barely visible. It vanished completely at the exact moment two women walked into the kitchen to announce Granny's passing.

Another story Alyce Faye relates in her book recalls the death of her grandfather. The death of Grandpa Huge was foretold by a strange dog that howled outside the window for two nights in a row at precisely two o'clock in the morning.

The third night, Grandpa Huge passed on at two o'clock. The night before her Grandpa O'Dell died, the rocking chair in the living room started to rock for no reason. Call these events strange coincidences, if you will. But keep reading. You may become a believer yet.

Grant County Token of Impending Death

One story told to a West Virginia resident by his father illustrates this belief in tokens or omens as related to coming death. This story took place in Iman Hollow, Grant County in the late 1940's before the storyteller's parents had electricity in their two-story farmhouse. The story begins on a bright moonlit fall night when his father could not sleep. He quietly got up and went downstairs to sit at the table and smoke a cigarette until he got sleepy. As he was sitting there, he suddenly saw a man's dark figure walk by the living room window. His father wasn't alarmed as he thought it was his wife's brother, Homer. His brother-in-law sometimes had one too many and was in the habit of stopping at his sister's house to sleep it off. He would knock on the door and holler his name out until they would come down and let him in for the night. (Even though no one ever locked their doors back then, he was gentleman enough to wait until someone came downstairs to open the door for him!)

Our storyteller recounts how his father got his flashlight and waited for Homer to knock and announce his presence. Silence. Then, the doorknob began to slowly turn. It turned half-way – not far enough to open the door. By that time, his father knew whoever was entering the kitchen was not his brother-in-law, so he quickly scrambled behind the door and raised his flashlight high in the air to use as a weapon. The doorknob slowly returned to its starting position as if someone had started to come in and then changed his mind. His father went outside and looked around the house and yard with his flashlight in readiness if he needed a weapon. Nothing and no one was to be found. The storyteller's father said how puzzled he was because he was positive someone had passed by the window in the bright moonlight.

A week or so later, our storyteller's grandfather, who lived two hollows over in Hinkle Hollow, strolled out onto the porch of his house. He dipped some snuff and turned around to go back into his house. As he took hold of the door knob and started to turn it, he had a massive heart attack and was dead before he hit the porch floor. Our storyteller said that his father always believed the dark figure he saw on that bright moonlit night and the turning of the door knob was a token of his father's death.

The Banshee – Harbinger of Death

A darker and slightly more sinister part of West Virginia's folklore came across the Atlantic Ocean as part of the region's Scotch-Irish heritage – the cry of the Banshee. The early Anglo-Celtic settlers of Appalachia had a deep and intimate belief in spirit beings such as fairies and the wee people, or leprechauns – mischievous magical spirit beings that help humans in time of trouble. However, the first traveling clergy in West Virginia discouraged all talk about these spirit beings by saying they were evil. After these staunch clerical admonitions against belief in the spirit beings, the first settlers to the Appalachians were reluctant to speak of them. Later groups of migrants into West Virginia, however, were encouraged by the Catholic priests to view the wee people as harmless supernatural beings – the substance of stories and legends. Sadly, by this time the stories about fairies and other spirit beings were already starting to lose their importance and thus, disappear from the folk culture. For this reason, stories about leprechauns and fairies have all but disappeared from the oral tradition in West Virginia.

However, one belief in spirit beings - the Banshee - seems to have survived.

Banshee comes from the word *van* which means "the Woman- the Beautiful," which is also the root word for *Venus*. Banshee means "the woman of the fairy race." The Ban-Sidhe was the spirit of death – the most feared and scary of the powers wielded by the fairies, and Leanan Sidhe was the spirit of life from which all musical and poetic inspiration came. It was believed that only certain families had a connection with these spirits. Persons who exhibited the fairy gifts of poetry and music were believed to walk closely with the spirit world. Poetry and prophecy were attributes of the spirit of life, Leanan Sidhe, while premonitions and warnings of death belonged to the spirit of death – the Banshee.

The Banshee brings an omen of death and doom to those of Irish or Scottish birthright. She is a supernatural being who typically rides a white horse and crosses water to announce the coming death of a family member with her shrill keening or crying for the dead. Sometimes the sound heard is a wild plaintive singing and other times a shrill, unearthly shriek that raises the hair on the back of one's neck. The Irish Banshee is slightly different than the Scottish one, but they both served the purpose of warning of impending death. The Irish Banshee appears to resemble a pretty young woman dressed in green with flowing red hair. Her eyes are blood-red from weeping for the dead. The Scottish Banshee, on the other hand, is dressed in grave clothes and wears a veil. Beneath the veil, she appears to resemble an old hag. Both Banshees are very selective in their clientele and only warn those of high-born families of a coming death. The Banshee is not limited to operations in the old country, either, as the following true story reveals.

The Marrtown Banshee

Marrtown, a small Wood County community near Parkersburg, has its own Banshee and the following story continues to be part of the folk culture of that region. Marrtown was settled in 1836 by a Scottish immigrant named Thomas Marr. Thomas married Mary in the fall of the year making her an autumn bride – a bad omen in the Scottish belief system. Perhaps this bad omen caused Mary to lose six of the eight babies she bore to Thomas in the coming years. The Civil War also took its toll on the Marrs as it did on many other families in West Virginia. Soldiers from both sides pillaged and stole crops and livestock from the Marrs. Public hangings and the death of two of their children to typhoid fever added yet more tragedy to the Marrs' lives. Finally, Thomas landed a job as night watchman at the toll bridge that crossed the Little Kanawha River between Parkersburg and Marrtown. All appeared to be well except for the fact that Thomas kept having a recurring strange encounter with a mysterious white figure on horseback.

Night after night, Thomas would meet up with this hooded figure of unknown gender riding a white horse. His encounters occurred at the same place on the road as he traveled to work every night. On a frigid February night, as Mary was awaiting Thomas' return from his job, the sound of a horse coming up the road to the house brought Mary to her window. Mary saw a white horse with a veiled rider approach and stop at the gate to her house. When Mary went outside to see what the rider wanted, the woman rider informed her to say her prayers. The Banshee told her Thomas had just died. After giving Mary the grim news, the white horse and rider galloped off and disappeared into the mist before they were out of sight. Within the hour, a messenger brought Mary the sad news that Thomas was dead.

Several stories have been written about how Thomas died that night but who really knows? In spite of how

Thomas met his end, one thing is agreed upon by most authorities and researchers-the Banshee paid a visit to the Marr clan and crossed water to do so. The Banshee of Marrtown is still reputed to ride and prophecy to those of pure Scottish blood that a death is coming to their family.

Doddridge County Banshee

Center Point, Doddridge County, also claims the dubious honor of having a local Banshee, or harbinger of death. During the summer of 1918, Pearl White and her grandmother saw and heard the Banshee of Center Point. It was a dark, moonless night and Pearl and her grandmother were on their way out the door to the outhouse before bed, when they heard a horse coming up the road. The hoofbeats were slow, steady, and measured, like the ticking of a clock. A pale veiled rider mounted on a white horse was coming slowly down their road towards the house. Pearl and her grandmother ran to the front porch to see what the nocturnal visitor wanted. The Banshee pointed at Pearl's grandmother and told her that one of her family would die that night. Then the eerie, high-pitched, keening cry of the Banshee sounded and the horse and rider galloped away.

Pearl and her grandmother ran inside just as Pearl's uncle collapsed and died from the Black Flu, a horrible sickness that was claiming many lives in the region at that time. Pearl and her grandmother never forgot the sights and sounds of the Banshee that night and Pearl, who grew up to become a well-known and very daring airplane stunt flyer, never overcame her fear of the dark.

Superstitions and Old Wives' Tales

While tokens and omens are specific "happenings" that predict a future event, other beliefs, called superstitions or old wives' tales, have also long been a part of the West

Virginian's life. Superstitions were used to explain the unexplainable. Motivated by fear of the unknown and the need to gain some measure of control over their lives, the early settlers lived and died following these beliefs and superstitions. These beliefs were held to be as important and powerful as religious rites and practices and were regarded as "gospel truth."

Superstitions are important contributors to the oral tradition of a culture because they are passed down from one generation to another by word of mouth. Sometimes one wonders what role self-fulfilling prophecy played in some of these beliefs and superstitions. Stories about these events have been passed down for generations in West Virginia as families tell and retell them to their children and grandchildren. Families sit by the fire late into the night discussing the strange things they have heard or seen and wondering what they mean.

Read them and see if YOU still believe in any of these superstitions.

Death –
- If you suddenly take a chill, someone just walked on your grave.
- The last person to leave a cemetery will be the next one to be buried there.
- Death comes in three's. If one person dies, two more will soon follow.
- If a dog howls outside your window, a death will soon occur in the family.
- If a bird flies into your house, someone in your family will die soon.
- If you hear a knock on your door and no one is there, someone in your family will soon die. It is a death knock.

- If you hear a ringing in your ears, you will soon hear of a death.

Good Luck –
- Finding a four-leaf clover.
- Hang a horseshoe over your front door to welcome good luck.
- Hang wind chimes outside your door to frighten away evil spirits.
- If your right hand itches, you will soon get money.
- If your left hand itches, you will soon receive a letter.
- If your feet itch, you are going to get a new pair of shoes or walk on strange ground.

Bad Luck –
- Giving an empty wallet as a gift.
- Make sure whoever hands you a knife, closes it and not you.
- Stepping on a sidewalk crack will break your mother's back!
- Friday the 13th is a day of bad luck.
- Spilled salt (unless you throw a pinch over your left shoulder).
- A sweet potato vine growing in the house that touches the floor.
- Two people making the same bed.
- A twitch in your right eye.
- Opening an umbrella indoors.
- Addressing a letter before you write it.
- Cats in the house of a family with a baby (it will draw the breath out of the baby).
- Using the same broom in a new house that you used in the old house.

Women and Work–
- It was bad luck for a woman to enter the coal mines. A man would soon lose his life.
- If a woman was part of a group of visitors to the mine, some miners would leave their jobs and head for the entrance. (Note: women often worked in the coal mines in England!)
- Coal mines were often haunted with ghosts of miners who had perished or women who were looking for their dead loved ones. Unexplained lights in the depths of these haunted mines lent credence to these beliefs.

Weather –
- Light brown wooly worms – easy winter. Dark brown wooly worms – hard winter.
- Bees building their nest in the ground – hard winter.
- Don't swim during the "dog days" of summer – wounds won't heal.
- Leaves turn over in the wind – rain is coming.
- Kittens are playful in the fall – bad weather is coming.
- If your beans burn, a storm's coming. (Water comes to a boil faster and boils away quicker when the barometric pressure drops – Granny was right!)

Marriage and Women's Events

Marriage, like death, has always been an important part of the tapestry of life in the Appalachians and there are many superstitions centered on marriage. For example, you never entered the church with your left foot because that would doom you to a bad marriage. Nor would a bride ever dream of making her own wedding dress because she could never hope to live long enough to wear it! The bride and groom would carry salt in their pocket, and the bride always wore something old, something new, something borrowed, something blue. If the bride wore yellow, she would marry a fine fellow. And you had better stay up all night during your wedding night, because the first one to fall asleep will also be the first one to die! Just don't dream of a wedding because that means there will be a separation.

Some interesting superstitions also surround the woman's "time of the month." Walking in the early morning dew at this time will surely bring on sickness or even an early death for a woman during her time of the month! And stay out of the garden, especially the cucumber patch, or the vines will rot! A woman or girl in the cucumber patch will prevent the cucumbers from pickling right and cause them to smell nasty. Tomatoes were also believed to be cursed by the "curse." However, it was fine to walk around the cabbages during this time – it would even encourage them to grow full heads! When canning time came, ladies were not even permitted in the kitchen to help with the canning if it was "their time." To be involved in the canning process would make the pickles spoil and otherwise ruin the process!

While it may seem nonsensical to believe that vegetables sense and respond to menstrual periods, most of us still refuse to open an umbrella in the house or walk under a ladder! Somewhere deep inside, we honor these old superstitions. Whatever the basis for these super-stitions, we cannot deny the influence they still hold in our lives. We may openly scoff at them as old wives' tales in the company of friends, but in the day-to-day living of our lives, they hold as much power as they ever did.

Chapter 2

Ramps, Greens, and Lots of Beans

Food has always been an important part of Appalachian culture. The earliest settlers to these scenic mountains found a wealth of fruits, nuts, berries, herbs, and wildlife with which to sustain life. The wide variety of available foods was only limited by the settlers' ability to preserve the surplus for the cold winter months. As we will soon discover, several ingenious methods of food preservation and storage were utilized to ensure enough food for survival.

The old-timers depended on the land for most of their diet. They imported very few foods but chose instead to live on what they could grow, gather, or kill. Early settlers had no choice but to take what nature provided. Canning and preserving foods seems old-fashioned to us now, but before these forms of food preservation were discovered, the first settlers could only dry or pickle a few foods. Most fruits and vegetables were seasonal and could not be saved for winter use. Cornmeal and salt pork were winter menu staples. Sometimes they were livened up with dried fruits such as apples or dried vegetables like green beans, called "leather britches." More often than not, however, the early settlers craved a taste of something green by the time spring approached. Their bodies were on the verge of scurvy and malnutrition and the early spring snows melted to reveal tasty ramps and other early greens!

It should be noted, however, that when we talk about the foods of West Virginia in this chapter, we are discussing traditional foods rather than the modern-day foods that make up the basis of the typical West Virginian's diet. Studies within the state and the southern Appalachian region seem to point out that fast food has finally conquered the deepest coves and reached the highest peaks of the Appalachian Mountains of West Virginia. Today, it seems McDonald's and Little Debbie cakes have infiltrated the menu in many families. Convenience foods such as canned soup and white "loaf bread" have taken a prominent place on the average table in West Virginia. Hot dogs and pickled pork products are popular food items throughout Appalachia and the traditional greens and beans in this chapter are no longer the mainstay of the average West Virginian's diet. However, as a way of preserving the traditional West Virginia folk ways and encouraging the future generations to rethink their diets, perhaps this chapter will serve a broader purpose than as just a recitation of culinary history.

Meals in Appalachia

Meals in the mountains used to consist of a hearty breakfast to start the work day, followed by a substantial noontime dinner to energize one to finish his or her work, and then a light supper as one started to prepare for a good night's rest. Mike's Uncle Claud lived with his grandparents on the banks of the Elk River in Duck (Villa Nova) for a season in 1937 or thereabouts. He recalls that his grandmother always cooked a large and varied assortment of foods for breakfast. This large meal was one of two major meals she cooked every day. If she had eggs or milk that needed to be used, she would bake custard pies for breakfast. The meal we now call lunch, eaten in the middle of the day, was traditionally referred to as "dinner" and was also a generous meal. Uncle Claud mentions that supper (now referred to as "dinner") was a modest meal and speculates the reason might have been because it was difficult to wash the dishes by kerosene lamp. In my travels around West Virginia today, I rarely hear the noon meal called "dinner" as most folks prefer the modern terminology – lunch. The evening meal is still referred to as "supper" in some hills and hollows, but the modern term – dinner – is becoming more widely used.

Ramps – The Lily of West Virginia's Valley

Springtime is a cause for great exultation in West Virginia. Spring means winter is behind us and ramp season is just ahead! The old saying that ramps are not for ladies or those who court them is just not true! I have witnessed many a gal enjoying the annual local ramp fest with her sweetheart. I think the secret is for both parties to enjoy ramps equally and not just one party to indulge.

While ramps are certainly a West Virginia delicacy, they are not for the faint of heart. They are tasty and strong-flavored and, if one eats enough of them, their odor comes out the pores and sweat glands for everyone around you to enjoy! Even before buds swell and leaves appear in the woods, ramps are ready to be dug and ramp suppers are being advertised in the local newspapers.

Ramps (Allium tricoccum), or wild leek, belong to the same family as onions, garlic, and chives. There are two versions of the name "ramps," both derived in the British Isles. A plant related to the ramp, *A. ursinum,* was called "ramson" because it appeared during the sign of the ram (Aries) between March 20 and April 20. Another prevalent theory claims that the English folk name "ramsen" referenced the Old English word for wild garlic, "hramsa." The early settlers to West Virginia were largely from the British Isles so when they discovered these garlic-like onion plants growing wild, they called them "ramsen" which was later shortened to ramps.

The early West Virginia settlers found the Native Americans' use of the ramp as a cure for colds and coughs handy. Native Americans also used the ramp juice as a poultice to relieve the sharp pain and itch of bee stings. Early settlers to West Virginia regarded ramps as a spring tonic and ate them to purge the body of accumulated toxins and cleanse the blood. Onions and garlic are now shown to be a great source of Vitamin C and a fatty acid called prostaglandin A that helps lower high blood pressure. Somehow the early West Virginian settlers intuitively knew the value of this odiferous root. West Virginia writer Alyce Faye Bragg writes in her book H*omesick for the Hills*, that "a hearty ramp dinner is as necessary to springtime as sassafras tea and will tone a sluggish system dulled by wintertime."

Whether used as a medicinal or an addition to the diet, West Virginians learn early to appreciate the strong pungent taste and aroma of the ramp. Often called a cross between garlic and onion, the ramp is eaten raw by the bold and hearty eater but is more often enjoyed in its cooked form as an addition to potato or meat dishes. Both the bulbs and the greens can be cooked. Many folks fry them with potatoes in bacon grease and sometimes add eggs to the mix.

Ramp suppers often feature ramps as an accompaniment to a smorgasbord of other entrees such as ham, chicken, cornbread and beans, salads of every kind, deviled eggs, and meatloaf. High-end eateries in big cities now feature ramps on their menus and open-air markets in fancy neighborhoods keep a steady supply for their clients. You can move away from West Virginia geographically but you can never move away from it culturally.

Where do ramps grow? How are they harvested? It's hard, muddy, and often chilly work to harvest enough ramps for a "mess" or a "feed." Ramps are bulbous, lily-like plants that grow in the moist deep woods and hillsides of the Appalachians. Folks start searching for them early in the spring because they are tastiest just after the shoots poke through the ground. The leaves resemble those of lily-of-the-valley – smooth, flat, and broad with magenta striping rising from the forest floor. They can grow to a height of 8 to 12 inches and spread rapidly to cover an entire hillside. Ramp diggers must dig ramps out of the cold, muddy ground and place them tenderly in burlap bags that must be dragged behind them as they continue their harvesting.

Some states, such as North Carolina, are concerned about a shortage of the plants and are charging ramp diggers a per-pound fee. Between 40 and 80 ramps constitute a pound and some ramps festivals, such as the one held annually in Richwood, West Virginia, use as much as 2,000 pounds of ramps. At this rate, are ramps becoming endangered as a natural plant in West Virginia? Should they come under U.S. Forest Service regulation as in North Carolina? It's a hard call to make!

Ramp-eating etiquette says that everyone eats them or no one eats them because of the bad breath and body odor problems they cause. Common knowledge in West Virginia says that those who eat ramps cannot smell themselves or others who also enjoy eating them. Abstinence from ramps is usually not a problem because, by the time spring rolls around the green hills of West Virginia, every person is craving these tasty gems and no one passes on them at the table. An old friend of mine from West Virginia told me that his school teacher always warned the students that everyone had to eat ramps or they would be sent home. He said that was because if you didn't eat them, you couldn't tolerate the stink that emanated from those who did.

Almost every community in West Virginia hosts ramp suppers or ramp festivals every spring. These ramp festivals have even drawn national media coverage as a PBS documentary, "King of Stink" and other media coverage. West Virginia cannot claim exclusivity to love of the ramp – other states in the southern Appalachian region such as Tennessee, North Carolina, and Virginia also enjoy digging and eating the ramp. Richwood, West Virginia does claim to hold the title of "Ramp Capital of the World" but ramp festivals and suppers are held in several other states and many of their place names include the word "ramp," signifying its importance in local folk culture.

Greens - Vitamins with Leaves

In the past, people from outside the Appalachian region associated a diet that included greens with poverty or a poor diet. Nowadays, however, medical science and nutritionists extol the virtues of eating these dark, leafy greens. "Greens" refer to a variety of green, leafy vegetables that include dandelion, turnip greens, cabbage, and wild greens such as poke sallet. (Collard greens are found predominantly in the Deep South but West Virginians have been known to grow and enjoy a "mess" of these tasty greens, too!) After a long, cold winter of dried meats and canned vegetables, fresh greens were always a welcome addition to the diet. Full of vitamins and minerals, these greens were eaten fresh and raw or cooked tender with onions and bacon drippings.

My grandpa used to pick dandelion greens early in the spring while they were tender and young. He claimed they "cleansed the blood" and, along with sassafras tea, were a necessary spring tonic. Dandelions are a "bitter" green and should be picked before they bud. To enjoy a mess of fresh dandelion greens, pick them and wash carefully. The boiled dressing that tops them off consists of eggs, vinegar, sugar, and milk or water. My mother always included a bit of mustard which "broke the bitterness" she said. Toss the greens lightly in the skillet with this dressing and get ready for something good! For a real treat, fry some bacon in the skillet before you prepare the dandelion greens. The bacon grease adds a good flavor to the dish. West Virginia columnist and author, Alice Faye Bragg of Clay County, writes she likes dandelion greens added to mixed wild greens and cooked until just a little tender. Endive, also considered a "bitter" green, can be used if fresh dandelion greens are not available.

Wilted lettuce or "killed lettuce" is also a springtime dish that celebrates the fresh, new lettuces that are usually the first produce harvested from a West Virginia garden. Wilted lettuce is picked fresh and topped with chopped green onions (also fresh from the garden) and a dressing made of hot bacon grease and vinegar. This dish is especially tasty when a pinch of sugar is added to the dressing and pieces of bacon are also included. The dressing is added right before serving and wilts the lettuce immediately! A Preston County cook recommends covering the salad dish with the hot skillet for a few minutes to complete the wilting process. Occasionally, chopped hard-cooked eggs will be added to this salad.

Polk (poke) sallet is a delicious wild green that was once a staple in the diet of any West Virginian. The roots of pokeweed are poisonous but the young leaves and stems are edible. Poke berries were traditionally used for medicinal purposes, but are rarely utilized these days. To prepare polk (poke) sallet, one native says you must boil it four or five times, discarding the water each time to get rid of the poisons in the sallet. Then you fry it in the skillet with bacon drippings and enjoy!

Other edible wild greens that are still gathered in April and enjoyed include turkey wing, bird tongue, goosegrass, purslane, thistle, narrow dock, rollvuncel, and lamb's quarter. They are best washed, parboiled, and fried in butter like fresh spinach. Once West Virginia families used to gather these wild greens every spring but now only a few isolated families even recognize them.

The water in which greens are cooked is called "pot liquor" and is full of vitamins and minerals cooked out of the greens. Women who had trouble getting pregnant were advised to drink pot liquor by the cup and it usually worked!

Soupbeans and Cornbread – Yum!!

West Virginians love their beans and what a variety of beans there are! Some common beans grown and eaten include navy beans, white beans, lima beans, pinto beans, October beans, green beans, and snap beans. In this category of staple foods we should also include the wide variety of pea's grown and eaten – green, field, and black-eyed, to name just a few. Beans and peas are starchy proteins that can be eaten fresh or dried and are usually cooked with bacon, salt pork, or ham. Beans have long served as the staple of the traditional West Virginia diet and are possibly the best food to serve at a fundraiser for the volunteer fire department. Few folks will turn down the chance for a heaping bowl of soupbeans and cornbread with all the trimmings.

When I was first married, my husband and I set up housekeeping next-door to his grandmother – called Grandma Bessie by family and neighbors alike. Grandma Bessie was a tiny woman not more than 4'10" tall and thin as a rail. She always wore a dress and apron and ate like a bird – nibbling seeds, nuts, and raisins all day long. Because she was a Mormon, Grandma Bessie abstained from tobacco, liquor, caffeine, and ate a very healthy diet. We always knew when soup beans and corn bread were on the menu at her house, because smoke would be pouring out her back door by noon! Grandma Bessie would often get in her beat-up, old station wagon and head over the 5th Street Bridge into Parkersburg to go shopping, forgetting her pot of soup beans on the stove. Many is the time I would walk in and rescue that pot of blackened beans and turn the fire off under them!

Old-timers say it's going to rain if the soupbeans burn or come close to burning. After pooh-poohing this as an old-wives tale, I finally learned that this is a scientific fact. As the barometric pressure drops, water comes to a boil quicker and boils away faster thus placing many a pot of soupbeans in jeopardy of a good scorch.

When I moved to West Virginia in the 1970's, I heard people refer to their favorite meal of "soup beans and cornbread." Born and raised in northern Pennsylvania, I had no idea what "soup beans and cornbread" referenced. "Beans" back home usually referred to green beans or lima beans cooked fresh with ham and onions in the summer or canned in quart jars for winter. However, in West Virginia, "soup beans" are pinto beans, white beans, or great northern beans cooked with onion and ham and served with cornbread. Often the cornbread is eaten crumbled up in the soup beans with green onions chopped and sprinkled on top. Cornbread is usually served with butter and honey as a side accompaniment to complete the meal, too. I make my cornbread sweet like the johnnycake my mother made at home, but my father-in-law said it should not be sweet and refused it at my table. My husband, who grew up in rural Ritchie County, said some of his friends in the Ellenboro grade school would not eat lunch at school unless "soup beans and cornbread" was on the lunch menu (and it appeared often)!

Cornbread is traditionally made in a cast iron skillet on top of the stove. All traditional Appalachian breads are cooked on top of the stove. Interestingly, this is part of the Scotch-Irish (Celtic) heritage of the region. Anglo-Saxons (English), German, and Mediterranean folks have always baked bread in ovens but the Celts baked all their varieties of bread on top of the stove or in the open fireplace. It was not until after the Civil War that the settlers of Appalachia adopted the use of the oven from the Pennsylvania Dutch (Pennsylvania Deutsch or Pennsylvania German) settlers. Their first oven - the Dutch oven - replaced the open fireplace.

Green beans have always been a versatile bean for West Virginians. Patricia Samples Workman describes her husband's family practice of stringing green beans with a needle and a two-or-three-foot long thread. These "high-strung" beans were hung in the sun on the porch to dry for the long winter months ahead. When dried, they were called "leather britches" and were stored for winter use. After cooking for several hours with water and a piece of fat pork, these dried green beans made a tasty and satisfying warm meal. Green beans are still a favorite vegetable in West Virginia and are almost always cooked with fat back or bacon grease. I include red potatoes and lots of onion in mine and never have left-over's!

Beans are truly a staple of a hearty country diet and full of B vitamins and fiber. With all the processed foods we fill up on these days, it isn't any wonder we come down with so many ailments from heart disease to cancers of all kinds. We need to get back to our roots – I mean our beans!

Mushrooms - Mollymoochers, Muggles, and Merkels!

Another delicacy of the hills and woodlands of West Virginia can only be found by rooting around among the dead, brown leaves leftover from last fall. As early settlers to West Virginia may have learned the hard way, most of the 1,700 or so mushrooms that grow wild in the state are tasty and harmless, **but** a few are toxic and deadly. The lush rainfall and widespread forests of West Virginia are fertile growing sites for the 1,700 or so delicious mushroom species that grow here.

By far the favorite of most fungi hunters, the morel (*Morchella* spp), or "haystack mushroom" comes in about six different varieties and can be harvested between the middle of April and the middle of May. Morels are generally called molly moochers, muggles, sponges, dry-land fish, haystacks, and merkels, and always have ridges or pits on their heads. They can be found under elms that are dying but never under conifers. If you scout an area a year or two following a forest fire, you should find lots of yellow and black morels growing. Most dedicated fungi hunters will not give away their prized morel territory so don't bother asking!

The yellow morel, or honeycomb morel, is often found where an old apple, cherry, or pear orchard once existed. They also grow under poplar trees and thrive in burned-out areas. Don't mix this morel up with the "false" morel. The best way to tell the difference is to cut the false morel open. An edible morel will be hollow inside but the false morel contains chambers and is thick and short-stemmed.

Some people claim you should not soak mushrooms in water but should only wipe them clean with a moistened paper towel. The exception to this rule is the morel. Morels **must** be soaked overnight in salt water with the water changed often. A tiny insect infests wild morels and the salt water soak will drive him out and to the top of the water bath where he can be discarded and not eaten!

Most folks I know drain the water off the morels and sauté them in bacon grease or a bit of butter. Of course, you can stuff them with bread dressing, deep fry them in batter, or slice them raw on salad just like you would any other mushroom.

The Golden Chanterelle (*Canthatellus cibarious*) is also a delicious mushroom with a fruity apricot-like aroma. Be careful not to mistake it for the poisonous jack-o-lantern mushroom (*Omphalotus olearius*) as both are bright orange. Severe cramps, diarrhea, and vomiting follow ingestion of the jack-o-lantern mushroom so look closely for its sharp gills growing directly out of wood and avoid it at all costs! King Bolete (*Boletus edulis*) is one of the best edible mushrooms in the world. It looks like a typical mushroom with a swollen stem or base and is usually found under conifers, especially spruce in the summer and fall. With its nutty taste and pleasant smell, it is easy to see why cooks all over the world are crazy about these fungi!

Mushroom hunting is a fun and highly rewarding hobby but must be approached with great caution. There are some fatally poisonous mushrooms native to West Virginia. One such killer -the pure-white pristinely virginal Destroying Angel (*Amanita virosa*) grows in the summer and early fall and is deadly poisonous. It contains a cyclopeptide called amanitin which kills liver cells and causes liver failure. It is usually found near oaks and is very common and widespread in North America and often the reason for poisoning fatalities in this country.

Please be careful! Mushrooms are a fascinating subject but not for the unschooled. Please take a seasoned mycologist, or mushroom expert, with you into the woods of West Virginia if you are anxious to harvest these local delights and are not absolutely a seasoned harvester yourself. Several annual mushroom hunts occur throughout West Virginia and mycology clubs are quite active here due to the state's optimum conditions for mushroom growth. Mushrooms are easily misidentified - especially those specimens tampered with by animals and the weather.

Never depend on a book of photographs to identify mushrooms as there are several characteristics that must **all** be checked and verified to safely identify edible mushrooms. The three main characteristics used to identify mushrooms are taste, color, and odor, but there are numerous nuances to these three categories. Never swallow a bite of mushroom that you taste. Always keep a portion of any mushroom you eat in a safe place, in case you start to exhibit symptoms of poisoning. If you become ill, you can give the doctor a sample of the mushroom for positive identification and accurate diagnosis and treatment.

Cat Head Biscuits – The Cat's Meow!

Biscuits have always been a staple of breakfast in West Virginia. Topped with gravy, butter and honey, or creamed tomatoes, there is nothing better with ham and eggs for breakfast. Aptly named because a fluffy delectable biscuit is as big as a cat's head, these can be eaten hot out of the oven with gravy, butter, honey, molasses, or strawberry jam. Sawmill gravy is a white gravy made from sausage or bacon drippings, white flour, and milk. Redeye gravy is also a tasty topping for cat head biscuits. It's made of hot black coffee stirred into the same pan in which you just fried up some ham. Add white flour to thicken and you have a lovely topping for biscuits, grits, or even eggs.

A good friend of mine shared her old family recipe for prize-winning cat head biscuits along with some very important directions for successful baking. First, you combine 2 cups of self-rising flour, one cup of buttermilk, and a walnut-sized lump of shortening, lard, or real butter (not a spread from a bowl) in a large mixing bowl. My friend puts the flour in the bowl first and makes a hole in the center of it. She puts the shortening in the hole and some of the milk and starts blending this mixture with a large wooden spoon. She adds the remainder of the milk gradually as she goes until soft dough is formed. DO NOT OVERBEAT! Over-beating and over-handling biscuit dough at any stage of the process will make the biscuits tough and chewy – not light and fluffy.

Once the dough is formed, roll it out onto a piece of floured waxed paper. Pat it down gently to a thickness of an inch and a half. Cut the biscuits from the dough with a biscuit cutter. I use the top of a drinking glass dipped in flour. Place the biscuits close together, sides touching, in a greased metal or glass baking pan. If they are crowded in the pan, they will rise up – not out- and you will get a light, fluffy product with soft, moist sides. Place the biscuit pan in a hot, 400 degree oven and bake just until the tops are golden brown and the insides are baked through. The timing is crucial because biscuits should never be "raw" inside, nor should they be brown and crunchy on top! Brush the tops with melted butter and enjoy!

An Apple a Day Keeps the Doctor Away

Few fruits are as versatile and popular as the much-loved apple. Traditionally, fall apples were preserved in two ways for winter munching. Apples were often sliced and strung on thread to dry in the sun. Dried apple pies were made out of these in the winter and were a welcome addition to the dried beans and smoked meats. "Holing the apples" was the second way of saving apples for winter eating. A hole was dug in the garden, the apples placed in it, and dirt and straw piled on top. When mother wanted a treat for the children, she would have one of them dig a few up and carefully re-cover the rest for another time.

Apple stack cake made from dried apples has always been one of West Virginia's most-loved desserts. Traditionally, it was usually reserved for a very special occasion because of the time and work involved in putting it together. This special cake is made of up to twelve thin layers held together with cooked dried apples sweetened with molasses or sorghum syrup and spiced with cinnamon and ginger. This cake is best when left to "settle" a few days while the thick, rich apple filling soaks down through the many layers. It should be kept in the refrigerator or a cool place until gone.

Odds 'n Ends

Cole slaw or "slaw" is a regional favorite choice as a salad accompaniment to any hot cooked meal in West Virginia. In fact, a recent survey taken by Barbara Shortridge, a geographer, showed that coleslaw is not only the top choice of West Virginians for a salad – it is universally a top pick throughout all of the Appalachian states (West Virginia, Alabama, Georgia, Kentucky, Tennessee, North Carolina and Virginia). Tossed salad also ranks high in West Virginia and sliced tomatoes were also a popular accompaniment to meals – especially breakfast.

Gravy bread – bread on a plate covered with brown gravy- was a favorite Sunday night supper dish for me as a child. One friend called it "poor man's gravy" or "poor-do" and said her mother often made it with bacon grease, flour, and milk and served it for breakfast. Today, I add fried bulk pork sausage and serve it over fluffy hot biscuits. We call it "biscuits and gravy" and there is not a finer way to start the day in my estimation! Some country-style family restaurants serve a good rendition of this family favorite on their menus. Speaking of biscuits, some folks liked to eat "soakies" – hot, buttered biscuit crust covered with hot coffee and cream. My Grandmother Shoup poured her breakfast coffee on her bowl of Wheaties – her version of "soakies," I guess.

My mother often made us cottage pudding for a special treat. Cottage pudding wasn't really a pudding – it was a made-from-scratch white cake topped with hard sauce. Hard sauce was a warm, rich, sweet raison sauce that literally made the cake melt in your mouth. I remember she baked this tasty treat on rainy summer days or cold, snowy days when I was a child. Those days just called for a warm oven and a special treat, I think.

Top-ranked desserts among those I have surveyed are usually made of fruit. This only makes sense as the lush humid climate of West Virginia's hills and valleys is ideal for growing fruits such as apples, peaches, and plums, and a large variety of berries. Berry cobblers are high on everyone's list with hot blackberry cobbler usually named the all-time favorite. This cobbler is served warm with milk poured over it but vanilla ice cream on hot blackberry cobbler is also very tasty. Strawberry shortcake is very popular in the early summer and pineapple upside-down cake is still Aunt Pauline's favorite at family get-togethers!

Food was important to the early inhabitants of the Appalachians but the ability to use the gifts of Nature as a cure for ailments was equally important. In a world where doctors and hospitals were virtually nonexistent, the early mountain dweller had to use the herbs, roots, and barks of the forest to facilitate a cure. These ingredients were often combined with chants and other rituals as you will see in the next chapter – Folk Remedies and Healing.

Chapter 3

Folk Remedies and Healing

Early settlers in the Appalachian Mountains had to depend on home remedies, tonics, and folk healers because of the shortage of trained doctors. The state of West Virginia did not even support a fully accredited, degree-conferring public institution to train doctors until 1962 although West Virginia University had a College of Medicine that functioned as a non-accredited type of medical program from 1902 until 1911.

The practice of healing with herbs and natural cures is generally passed down in families with the child learning the identification of herbs and where to find them from his or her elders. Folk healers know where to locate the various herbs, roots, leaves, and barks they employ in their healing practice but today many bemoan the increasing scarcity of these items. Folk healing is still practiced in the Appalachian region; however, today most individuals who go to folk healers or use their remedies do so in conjunction with modern medicine. It is not a question of one or the other but rather a dependence on whichever one works best for the purpose. Herbs and natural remedies are often used to handle the day-to-day minor complaints of life but when a diagnosis of serious illness is made, people usually have no trouble seeking out the best treatment modern medicine has to offer.

Certain home remedies had been handed down for several generations and were trusted and used by the first folks to settle these mountains. Some scholars believe a few of these remedies can be traced back to Europe and the old custom of brewing potions and elixirs for witchcraft practices. In addition, some remedies were devised in the mountains of West Virginia as the early settlers experimented with the providence of nature.

Experience is usually the best teacher – even in home remedies. The early settlers probably tried one concoction after another, boiling tea from an assortment of roots, twigs, and berries, until something actually worked (or fatally, did not work, as the case may be). Most home remedies involved the use of herbs. If all else failed, the jug of liquor which contained the herbs could be counted on to soothe the pain!

Although living in the relatively pure and unspoiled Appalachian Mountains was far healthier than dwelling in the industrially-polluted, disease-ridden cities of the day, the early inhabitants of West Virginia still had sicknesses and ailments. Families would have to deal with accidents and illnesses the best way they could since formal medical care was virtually nonexistent. Just as people still believe in old wives tales and superstitions from past generations, they sometimes continue to turn to tried-and-true "home remedies" when all else fails. Since roughly one quarter of our modern-day medicines are derived from plants and barks found in nature, it is not that hard to understand our ancestors' dependence on these folk remedies for health and healing. The rich biodiversity of Appalachian hills and hollows created a veritable treasure trove of pharmaceuticals. Even in our advanced and modern society, today's visiting nurses and other health professionals in West Virginia claim that the lingering on of the "old ways" sometimes interferes with their patient care.

The number "3" appears often in folk healing and some scholars think this reflects the importance of the Holy

Trinity of Father, Son, and Holy Ghost in everyday mountain life. Others believe the trichotomy replicates the nuclear family structure of father, mother, and child. The importance of the number "3" in Appalachian folk healing is well-documented regardless of its origins and rituals, charms, and incantations are almost always repeated three times in order to work.

Frequently, sympathetic magic was used in Appalachian healing cures. For example, if you wanted to cut or stop the pains of a woman in labor, you would place an ax under her bed. Passing a child from mother to father three times would cause the child to "pass" from a state of sickness to a state of health. Another cure based on the belief of "passing" was the placing of a paper bag (poke) with stones equal to the number of warts one had along the side of the road. When a curious traveler picked up the bag to peer inside, the warts would "pass" to them.

This chapter will describe a few old home remedies that are still in use today. These have been gleaned from various first-person accounts shared with myself and others. Some of these remedies are developed from combinations of leaves, roots, bark, and berries while others are based on superstition and magic. A word of caution! Just because they are "natural," do not think that every berry, leaf, and root is healthy to ingest! We will begin this chapter with a few words of caution. I believe it is wise not to experiment in this realm without some foreknowledge, so please read and take to heart the following information.

Be Berry Careful with Berries!

While most wild berries are safe to eat both in their cooked and raw forms, there are some exceptions. One of my favorite berries to bake in a pie is the American black elderberry (*Sambucus nigra* L. ssp. *canadensis* (L.) R.

Bolli. These berries baked in a juicy pie or coaxed into a jug of wine can create a state of heavenly bliss! However, the elderberry in its raw state is toxic! Some believe even the slightly greenish immature elderberries are toxic and should not be eaten – cooked or raw.

Elderberries abound in late summer and grow abundantly in wet, swampy areas. The leaves, stems, twigs, roots and unripe berries of all elderberry varieties are toxic and can make a person very ill. I am very careful to even pick all the tiny red stems out of my pie berries before adding the sugar and cornstarch and top crust. When the clusters of berries hang heavy on their stems and are purple-black in color, the elderberries are sweet, juicy, and prime for picking and using for pies, wine, and jellies. As with most dark red and purple fruits, elderberries contain an abundance of antioxidants and are believed to boost immunity to sickness and disease by those who practice homeopathic medicine. Elderberries are also used in making liquor called "Sambuca."

Polk berries from the Pokeweed plant, *Phytolacca Americana*, are also deadly when eaten raw. They can be identified by their bright red stalks – nature's flag of warning. The berries hang in grape-like clusters and change color gradually as they mature from a pale green to a red and then dark purple when fully ripe. The entire pokeweed plant, but especially the berry, is poisonous in its raw state, and will cause vomiting and diarrhea. In fact, the Native Americans used the pokeweed plant as a purgative. They believed the violent vomiting and diarrhea it induced signified its ability to drive out evil spirits from an individual.

Although poke berries are very toxic – raw or cooked- to humans, birds absolutely love poke berries and can eat them without harm. Pokeweed contains two toxins that are deadly to mammals - phytolaccatoxin and phytolaccigenin. However, when birds eat the berries, the toxin-containing tiny seeds pass through their digestive systems and are eliminated whole. The poke plant is a wonderful source of bird food and multiplies rapidly in average soil so if you have a corner of the yard that you can allow it to take over, your bird buddies will really appreciate you.

The poke plant is also known as Inkberry because the berry juice was fermented and made into ink by early settlers. The United States Declaration of Independence was written in fermented pokeberry juice as well as many letters written home during the Civil War. The berries were also boiled and used as a brown dye by the early inhabitants of the mountains.

Appalachian cuisine has long ignored the cautions against eating parts of the pokeweed plant. Poke salat (salad) festivals are regularly held across the region every year and many folks gather to enjoy the delights of poke greens. Poke salat is made by boiling young pokeweed leaves three times to reduce the toxin and discarding the water after each boiling. Medical authorities strongly advise against eating pokeweed even after several boilings because the toxin is still present in small amounts. Folk healers and herbalists use parts of the pokeweed plant to facilitate healing but I do not advocate using any part of the plant as a cure. Great care and knowledge must be used in dealing with this plant and it is best left in the hands of herbalists and those skilled in homeopathic medicine.

Berry Good Berries!

Blackberries are especially good for your health and have one of the highest levels of antioxidants found in any fruit. There are approximately 20 species of edible blackberry (genus *Rubrus)* growing in West Virginia and they are all safe, sweet, and delicious for man and beast to eat. They are commonly regarded as the most abundant and valuable summer food for wildlife in West Virginia. Birds, black bear, rabbits, and raccoons all benefit from the blackberry as a source of food and cover. Small bird species use the dense bramble thickets as nesting sites. As a folk remedy, the berries or juice will cause diarrhea to stop quickly. Blackberries are still canned and eaten for their diarrhea-quelling properties. Blackberries contain large amounts of vitamins A and C, potassium, and bioflavonoids. Their healing and preventive qualities are numerous and include reducing the risk of cancer, reducing cholesterol levels, protection against heart disease, and slowing the ageing process. They are high in fiber, too, so they belong on every menu!

The small wild strawberries found growing wild in the hillside meadows of the Appalachian Mountains are ten times sweeter than the hard, crunchy golf ball-sized varieties found in the local grocery stores and have lots of vitamins, too. Strawberries contain pantothenic acid, or vitamin B^5, which very few fruits have. Pantothenic acid is needed to metabolize fats, proteins, and carbohydrates in our bodies. Strawberries also contain ellagic acid which is now widely believed by the medical community to stimulate certain cancer-fighting enzymes.

Mountain folk healers have long used the strawberry as a treatment for various skin conditions such as acne. A poultice of crushed strawberries will quickly relieve sunburn when applied to the affected skin. In addition, the strawberry's astringent properties were often used to eliminate freckles and whiten the skin. Strawberry leaves are also known as a great astringent and can be used when fresh or dry. Early settlers ate strawberries to relieve gastritis and diarrhea symptoms. After a bout of hepatitis, jaundice, or liver disease, strawberry leaves were used to aid in facilitating a quick recovery. A tonic wine made of wild strawberries can be made by steeping the berries in wine. The leaves are used to create an infusion that battles the irritating symptoms of diarrhea. Gastric inflammations, infections in the stomach, and jaundice all respond to the leaves of wild strawberries.

Are You Barking up the Right Tree?

    The original settlers of the Appalachian Mountains found a treasure chest cornucopia of trees in West Virginia's verdant forests when they arrived. Some of the trees were readily identified but new species had to be approached with caution and yet, excitement, at their potential powers. The Native Americans living in the region gradually were persuaded to share their healing secrets with these early settlers and the use of bark, leaves, and twigs to make medicinal teas became an invaluable part of Appalachian folk healing and culture.

    Bark, leaves, and twigs are still often boiled to make healing teas to soothe a variety of ailments. White and black willow bark and leaves were boiled into a tea to break a fever. This remedy worked well since willow contains a wealth of salicylic acid (aspirin)! The twigs and leaves of red cedar were boiled and the vapors inhaled to break-up the congestion of bronchitis. Yellow root, or goldenseal, tea was an instant cure for a sore throat and sweet goldenrod tea, tasting faintly of licorice, was the favored brew of the American Revolution. Asthma and hay fever sufferers benefited from brewing a tea from sumac leaves.

The Root of the Matter

    Roots had a purpose, too. Dandelion root was often dug, dried, and ground up for a coffee substitute. It is a member of the chicory family and it is used as the main ingredient in all coffees in most parts of the Deep South. The dandelion root, when added to coffee as an extract, served as a mild laxative, diuretic, and stomach aid, too. The roots of the rhubarb plant were often used as a laxative and additionally, as an astringent for the skin.

The Native Americans used another wonderful root – the red sassafras – to purify the blood and also to treat skin diseases and the ague. My grandfather always dug up some red sassafras root and brewed a spring tonic out of it. He claimed it thinned the blood and got rid of impurities that had been building-up through the winter. Sometimes old-timers will add some maple sap to sassafras tea to make it even tastier. The first settlers to these mountains brewed the sassafras roots with molasses to make a fermented beverage or beer. Sassafras tea makes a fine blood thinner in the spring and you will kick up your heels like a cow let out of the barn for the first time in months, but be warned! Do not drink this tea for more than a week as it contains volatile oils - mainly *safrole* - that may lead to liver cancer.

Granny's Herb Garden

Almost every herb in Granny's herb garden was brewed in water to form a tea. The heat of the hot water aided in releasing the herb's healing properties and the hot drink made for a more pleasant experience for the patient than a cold glass full of floating leaves. Peppermint and spearmint leaves were widely used as a tea to treat colic, dyspepsia, stomach aches, spasms, and nervous hysteria. Both mints grow in abundance along creek banks throughout the region and were gathered, dried, and stored for later use. My earliest memories of tummy aches as a child are flavored with the cups of aromatic peppermint tea my mother and grandmother brewed for me out of peppermint leaves. Colicky babies were fed a bottle of catnip tea and ginger tea settled the nausea of early pregnancy. Ground ivy tea soothes colicky babies with its mild tranquilizing effects. Menstrual cramps could be eased with pennyroyal leaves brewed up in a hot tea and a tea made from sage or the buds of the male fern would flush the tapeworms right out of your system. Marshmallow leaf tea was often used to treat urinary tract irritations.

Yarrow, or milfoil, was used as a painkiller and has properties similar to aspirin. It was also used to break a sweat during a cold and even as a cure for baldness! A strong tea made of yarrow stops the bleeding when placed on a wound. Jewelweed (touch-me-nots) brought relief from poison ivy rashes and stinging nettle irritations when the leaves were crushed and applied as a poultice.

Herbs used as seasonings and flavorings included horseradish which was very popular in flavoring meats and salads. The horseradish roots were ground up and mixed with sugar and vinegar to make a flavorful condiment. Ground mustard seed was also used to season food. The ground seeds were mixed into a paste with flour and water. When not used as a condiment, mustard seed was used as a poultice or plaster applied directly on the chest to fight colds, pneumonia, and headaches.

Many of the above-mentioned medical herbs were gathered and dried, and kept for use any time they were needed. Most of the herbs regularly used for healing had genuine virtue but some were merely plants that had no real medicinal use. These plants relied on superstition to give them value. Ginseng (*Panax quinquefolius*) is one such plant that is highly prized in the market but has little proven medicinal value. The word "panacea" is thought to be derived from ginseng's Latin name because this incredible plant is given credit for curing everything from shingles to cancer. While ginseng is reputed to be both a tonic for energy and an aphrodisiac, both these claims are largely untested in the scientific world. The harvesting and sale of ginseng has become a handy second income for some West Virginians who are out of work or otherwise need some extra money. The voracious ginseng market in China provides "sangers" with a ready buyer as the roots are regarded as man's most valuable medicine.

Cautions!!!

One might be tempted to set out looking for some of these herbs but this is not as easy as it sounds! Edible and medicinal herbs and plants are sometimes difficult to identify. I strongly recommend anyone interested in natural herbal remedies or folk healing to sign up for a community education workshop on the subject. Biologists and herbalists are trained and can teach you how to **safely** identify herbs commonly used for healing and health.

However, knowing that a few of you might be tempted and independent-minded, I will give you a few basic tenets of identification and use. Some herbs and plants are safe in small doses **only**. Examples of this are sheep sorrel and wood sorrel- both are high in oxalic acid and should be ingested in very small doses only. Avoid the parsnip family of plants, too. Cow parsley and water hemlock can both be toxic.

One last warning to those tempted to put some of these herbs in a pipe. Mike's Uncle Claud cautions to be careful what you smoke! When he was just a small school boy at the one-room school in Duck (Villa Nova), the older boys showed him how to smoke a plant called field blossom in a little pipe whittled out of an acorn. When his grandmother found out about his new habit, she warned him to stop or he would get yellow jaundice. The warning was enough to scare him into giving up this habit!

Magical Cures and Remedies

Appalachian folk healers believed that God provided everything we needed in this world through His bounty in nature. The cure for an ailment might often be found growing right next to the source of the ailment – Divine Providence! Many folk healers believe that God puts such bounty in the natural world for our use and good. They believe there is possibly a natural cure for every disease known to man (and then some) in the plants and trees of this world. Early settlers to the Appalachian Mountains practiced the doctrine of signatures in which they believe God gives us a clue, or sign, to a plant's latent medical use.

    The doctrine of signatures was widely espoused in Europe during the Middle Ages and can be traced back to the writings of Dioscorides, an ancient Greek botanist and physician. This form of magic held that a person or object could be supernaturally affected by an action done to an object representing the person or thing. For example, a plant that produced a flower resembling a human organ, such as the heart or lungs, was believed to be a healing herb for that organ. Lungwort - *Pulmonaria officinalis (Boraginaceae)* is an herb used to treat bronchitis and other pulmonary disorders. The wide, oval-shaped spotted leaves resemble the tissues of the lung. The white spots on the leaves were thought to resemble ulcers or sores on the lungs. *Pulmonaria* comes from the Latin word *pulmo* which means 'the lung' in English. As a result, the lungwort, and medicines prepared from its derivatives, was widely used in the Appalachian region to treat pulmonary disorders ranging from bronchitis to pneumonia. In a similar fashion, toothwort was thought to relieve toothaches and snakewort was thought to cure snakebite. Liverworts were thought to resemble the liver and are members of a group of herbs called *hepatics*, from the Latin *hepaticus* meaning "belonging to the liver." Liverworts were used to treat diseases of the liver. Today's science relegates the doctrine of signatures to a dusty top shelf by regarding the doctrine as nothing more than superstition. Scientists cannot find any connection between the herbs and the diseases they are purported to cure. Also, there is no medical evidence that the doctrine of signatures led to the discovery of medical uses of the plants. Jewelweed, often found growing next to poison ivy, is actually a potent natural cure for the ailment. In this case, the doctrine of signatures holds true. Just a coincidence? Perhaps and yet, when one lives in the mountains, one has a recognition that something stronger and more powerful than "chance" and coincidence is at work in your daily life.

The use of herbs as powerful defenses against the forces of evil is well-documented in Appalachian culture. Yarrow, Achillea millefolium, also called Devil's Plaything and Devil's Nettle, was said to be one of the devil's herbs and has been associated with magic and witchcraft. However, yarrow was often used as a charm to give protection against the very evil is was associated with. It was sprinkled across the threshold of a house to keep out evil influences and a bag of yarrow was often worn to guard against evil spells. Sometimes sprigs of yarrow were fastened to a baby's cradle to protect the infant from witches who might try to steal away its soul, which was considered a real possibility in cases where there had been a delay in baptizing the infant. Yarrow was also gathered on St. John's or Midsummer Eve (June 21, the summer solstice and a day of great magical power and significance) to be given to a woman in labor. She held a bunch of the herb pressed to her right side during childbirth, but it had to be taken away as soon as the child was born.

Sprigs of fresh basil and rosemary placed over windows and on their sills can protect the home from "haints" or evil spirits. You could also dry some basil and hang it over your doors and on the fireplace mantel to prevent evil spirits from entering your home through those portals, as well. Throw some basil and rosemary into the fire to further protect your home and bring happiness.

Sympathetic magic or the idea that "like cures like," was also prevalent in Appalachia. For example, one could cut the pain of a woman in childbirth by placing an axe under her bed. Another variation of this idea is that of "passing." It was believed that a child could be healed of the group or some other sickness by passing the child back and forth between the father and the mother. Passing involved going from one state to another, as from sickness to health. Usually, passing was performed three times since trichotomy, or the power thought to be held in the number three, was widely espoused in the mountains. Trichotomy is widely believed to be a result of the Christian belief in the Trinity – Father, Son, and Holy Spirit- a belief strongly followed in the Christian theology of the region. Illness was not the only commodity that could be transferred, or passed, from one to another. Older family members sometimes slept with young children in the hopes that the child's vitality and energy would "pass" to the older family member.

Not all knowledge of healing and remedies came across the Atlantic, however. When the early settlers moved into the region, they encountered the Cherokee and other Native American groups. The main impact the Cherokee folk medicine customs made on the early newcomers to the region was in passing on their knowledge of healing plants indigenous to the mountains. Both the Cherokee and the early settlers found the Appalachian Mountains to be "healing landscapes," in the words of anthropologist Anthony Cavendish in his book "Folk Medicine in Southern Appalachia." Over 2,500 different plant species call the biologically diverse Appalachian Mountains home with approximately 1,100 of these purported to possess healing properties. The mountain folk relied on a very small group of these 1,100 plants for healing remedies.

Sassafras, goldenseal, witch hazel, slippery elm, snakeroot, and boneset were just a few of the new plants the early settlers discovered in the Appalachians when they arrived. But they brought with them many plants from Europe that quickly naturalized in the fertile soils of America. Dandelion, horehounds, alfalfa, peppermint, feverfew, and St. Johnswort are just a few of the European plants introduced to the Appalachian region.

While the early setters brought with them the doctrine of signatures, the Cherokee used something very similar as well. For instance, if a plant produced a milky sap, it was used to treat a urinary tract illness that produced a milky discharge. Scholars believe these two systems of natural remedies developed separately and independent of each other. The Native Americans adopted several European herbs for their own use, too. Some of the plants they began using were tansy, catnip, burdock, and yarrow. The methods of administering medicinals were quite different when it came to the settlers and the Native Americans. The early settlers ingested their herbal teas or decoctions while the Native Americans preferred to blow their smoke onto the patient from a distance of three or four feet.

The Gift

Throughout the Appalachian region, there is still talk of a family member or individual who possesses "the gift." Individuals who possess the "gift of second sight," sometimes referred to simply as "the gift," are traditionally Appalachian women. The gift might be an ability to see the dead or simply possession of the ability to know things of which they should have no natural knowledge. This ability is most often inherited from the mother's side of the family. Tales and legends of second sight go back to the British Isles before the time of the European immigration to

Appalachia and many "seers" trace their gift back to that time.

Other folks thought to have special healing powers and other "extra" gifts were those born with a veil, or thin membrane also called a caul, over their face. Individuals with hazel eyes, or eyes with a different color surrounding the outer circle of the iris, were also thought to possess special curative powers as well as the ability to "know" things that most folks did not know. One widely –held belief in the hills of West Virginia was that the seventh sons of seventh sons had special powers that could heal persons suffering from thrush and mouth sores. It is not difficult to understand why people with "the gift" were sought after in the mountains. If you could gain a bit of knowledge about the unknown future that would give you "the jump" on your circumstances – why not?

Charming Blood

The idea of speaking words, or conjuring, to heal the sick was widespread throughout the Appalachians. One woman remembers her grandfather could conjure thrush and heal both mother and baby by speaking words over them. He told his granddaughter she could not do that, however, because she lacked sufficient faith. The belief in the power of the spoken word has deep roots in the religious faith of those living in the Appalachians. Perhaps this widespread faith and trust in the spoken word to heal and affect cures can also be traced to older beliefs in magic, spells, and incantations that the earliest settlers brought over from Europe and the British Isles.

Another superstition I have encountered many times concerns "charming blood" or stopping excessive bleeding and hemorrhaging through a simple incantation of a scripture. Not everyone possessed this gift or ability, however, but those who did were in great demand in the days when emergency rooms and hospitals were the luxury of city dwellers. The healer would repeat the injured person's name three times and then repeat the biblical passage from Ezekiel 16:6 (rcferred to as "the Blood Verse)." The verse says, ""And when I passed by thee, and saw thee polluted in thine own blood, I said unto thee when thou wast in thy blood, Live; yea, I said unto thee when thou wast in thy blood, Live." This procedure would be repeated twice over again (some say three times) and then the practitioner would say the complete name of the person who was bleeding and the bleeding would stop. The practitioner does not have to have any extra measure of faith or be without sin. The power of the Blood Verse overrides any deficiencies in the practitioner. Some folks claim only women can charm blood in men and only men in women but I have personally heard stories of an uncle charming the blood and staunching the flow of a young nephew, so I am uncertain about that claim. Another treatment to stop bleeding from a wound was to apply chimney soot to the cut. If just your nose was bleeding, however, you could easily cure it by pressing an iron key to the back of your neck!

  Another old remedy based on superstition deals with relieving the horrible pain of a toothache. Back when dental care was nonexistent and dentists rarely found, folks had to find ways to alleviate the mind-numbing pain of an abscessed or decayed tooth. The afflicted person was instructed to walk backward as many steps as the number of years of his age. Simple enough, you might say. However, the catch was that the person had to do so with a dead horse's jawbone in his mouth! Another toothache remedy claimed you could rub a splinter around the gum until you drew blood and then drive the splinter into the bark of a tree. The toothache would disappear after that procedure! A toothache in your left jaw can be cured by tying a string around the little toe of your right foot, and vice versa. And of course, the wise person always consults the almanac for phases of the moon and the position of the stars and astrological signs before having a tooth extracted.

Living close to nature has always had its threats and dangers. Snakes are in plentiful supply in the hills of West Virginia. If you were bitten by one, some folks claimed you should cut up the snake that bit you and apply its flesh to your snakebite. This supposedly would draw out the poison.

A favorite remedy for most ills was the jug of liquor in which herbs were mixed. The spirits were supposed to hasten the flow of blood and carry the virtue of the herbs to the affected parts promptly. They preserved the remedy indefinitely and stimulated the patient. But sometimes, as in snake bite, the remedy was worse than the disease.

If eating a healthy diet and partaking of folk remedies and cures did not keep the early settler alive, the next chapter would come in handy! Chapter 4 -Waking the Dead and Other Burial Customs – discusses death rituals practiced in the mountains of West Virginia.

Chapter 4

Waking the Dead and Other Burial Customs

Death in the Appalachian Mountains of West Virginia has always been accepted as a natural part of life. Much like the seasons that cycle through these mountains – sowing, watering, harvesting – the lives of mountain folk passed from birth to marriage to death with children, sickness, and hopefully, lots of good times, somewhere in the middle. Death was an accepted part of their lives. The casual acceptance of death is best found in how it was announced in a matter-of-fact way – "he jist took to his bed and up and made a die of it."

Long before funeral homes sprang up to service mountain families when death occurred, the family filled the need. In Appalachian communities throughout the nineteenth century, families prepared the deceased's body for viewing at home. Even when professional funeral parlors and undertakers were available during the late 1800's, most families felt they were better able to treat the corpse with the respect it was due than were strangers.

Well into the 20th century, in certain communities the funeral director's services were only needed to provide a casket for viewing purposes. For reasons unknown to me, some families did not permit their dead to be embalmed. Since the body was not embalmed, the burial was generally held the day following the death. On more than one occasion, the lack of embalming proved to be a blessing to the family as well as the one presumed to be deceased. On one such occasion, the funeral director was preparing to close the casket over the unembalmed person, as the viewing was over. He noticed the woman's chest expand as she took a deep breath. When he came to his senses again and was able to function, he put a mirror to her lips and pronounced her alive! The family rushed her to the hospital in a deep coma. The woman managed to live three more weeks before it really was her time to be buried.

Harry Franklin Shaw, a retired West Virginia mountain preacher, wrote in his memoirs about one funeral he was asked to preach long ago. He had just sat down to eat his supper on a cold, rainy night when a knock at the door brought him to his feet. A man who lived up a nearby holler told him his mother had died that morning and asked him to help with the arrangements and preach the funeral. Preacher Shaw drove to the family's house to help with the arrangements and found the deceased "laid out" in a small bedroom on an Army cot. She had her Sunday best outfit on and lay with her hands neatly folded at her waist. All the windows were open and the single gaslight quaked and wavered as the wind blew, casting wild shadows on the walls.

Shaw recounted that the woman's husband had cut a huge white oak tree shortly before his death 20 years ago. The lumber from the tree was earmarked for his casket with the remainder to be saved in the barn for his wife's casket when she departed. A grandson had found the lumber a few years ago and used it to build some new kitchen cabinets for his brand-new home. Family members drove to the grandson's house and dismantled the cabinets bringing the lumber back to build the woman's casket. Each piece of the coffin was carefully cut by hand, sanded, fitted, glued, drilled, and screwed together securely. Handles and hinges were purchased at the funeral home and fastened to the casket. It really looked professional by the time the men were done, Shaw relates.

The women of the family were sewing the casket liner as the men were working. They prepared a gray satin lining with cushions for the head and body to lie on. The next day the funeral director sent a hearse to pick up the body. He reminded Preacher Shaw that the day was warm and he shouldn't take too much time preaching. When he arrived at the church, it was already packed and a long line of mourners took their turns paying their last respects to the deceased. When everyone was finally seated, singing began followed by preaching and a final viewing. Dust to dust and ashes to ashes – another proud Appalachian saint goes on to meet their Maker!

Patricia Workman tells of her husband, Clennie's, memories of burials in Nicholas and Clay County in "Fond Recollections: My Memories of Clennie." He told her that when someone died, the family would build a simple wooden box of pine for the body. Members of the extended family would dig the person's grave and the burial would take place the next day. Smooth, flat field stones were used as grave markers for the head and foot of the grave and no names or dates were ever carved on the stones. What was the need for a fancy memorial or even a plaque with names and dates? The family knew who was buried where and that was the only thing that mattered.

"Waking" the Dead

The custom of viewing the deceased and paying respects to the grieving family in the home is commonly referred to as a wake or a "sitting up." The mountain folk of Appalachia brought this custom of staying with the deceased until burial from the British Isles. The term "wake" comes from the Anglo-Saxon word "lic" for "corpse," and means to watch or keep vigil. Many ancient groups have observed wakes, keeping watch over their dead to prevent unholy spirits from carrying the body off before burial and to stop wild animals from seizing the body and dragging it off. The wake also served another useful purpose in the mountains. The body had to be observed carefully for signs of life to ensure the person was actually dead.

The Appalachian wake was a festive time of celebration and dancing, drinking, and laughter as was the Irish custom of observance. The wake represented the last social fling of the deceased whose presence was symbolic of the fact that he was still very much a part of the community. While the deceased was no longer present in spirit, their body was still to be found with the living so the wake became the last social event for the departed. The newly deceased person was marking his or her final transition from life into death with this ceremony and the entire community usually participated. Friends and neighbors came to pay their final respects to the dead and give support and comfort to the grieving family. The wake also provided the family with a chance to adjust to the loss of their loved one before the body was placed in its final resting place in the ground.

When a death occurred, everyone in the community mobilized. The deceased was placed on a laying-out board or cooling board, as it was sometimes called, to keep the "cold death" or "stiffening" from occurring. This board could be a door taken off its hinges, an ironing board, or any lumber that provided a firm, straight, hard surface for laying out the body prior to rigor mortis. The cooling board was generally covered with a sheet or tablecloth. Strips of cloth or handkerchiefs were used to secure the jaw closed by wrapping the head securely from the jaws and up around the top of the head. The legs were tied together at the ankles. The body was also secured to the cooling board with cloth strips to prevent the corpse from sitting up and scaring the wits out of the living.

Family members prepared the body for the wake by washing it carefully with soap and water and placing it in Sunday church clothes. If the deceased did not have clothing suitable for burial, family members would contribute their own or a woman in the community would sew a new garment. Often, women would sew their own burial clothes and lay them away for when the time came to wear them. Women were traditionally buried in black or white and children were always buried in white. Men typically were buried in a white shirt, tie, and pants. No time was wasted in preparing the body as rigor mortis sets in immediately upon death and the necessity of clothing a body quickly while it could still be done was paramount.

As the body was being prepared for the wake, members of the community brought food to the home. Death, no matter how abrupt or unexpected, always came in the midst of life and the living required sustenance. Appalachian folk knew how important food is to any family or community gathering and they always made sure there was an ample supply of it available. Along with the food came support and comfort for the family in their time of loss. The rural isolation of their mountain surroundings created a need for this vital support network.

A bowl filled with salt and ashes was sometimes positioned under the cooling board to absorb disease and occasionally cedar chips, spicebush, or aromatic barks and spices were placed near the body to help mask any disagreeable odors. The church bell was tolled to announce the passing of the deceased with the number of times corresponding to the person's age. This practice crossed the Atlantic from Europe and the British Isles where ringing the bells was common practice to announce a death and to scare away the evil spirits.

Once the body was bathed and dressed, silver coins were placed on the eyes to keep them from opening. One of the worst insults to a person's character in the Appalachian

Mountains was to have someone say "he'd steal money off a dead man's eyes." The expression is still in use. It was widely believed that one should enter Heaven in humility and in a penitential attitude with closed eyes. If ones eyes were closed, God would note the deceased was seeking forgiveness of sins and view him or her with leniency. Silver coins were preferred for this purpose since copper pennies had a way of discoloring the skin with a greenish coloration. Soda or camphor-soaked rags were continuously applied to the face until viewing to prevent discoloration. The funeral service and burial took place the following day with no delay. The only occasion for delayed burial that I have found is when the ground was frozen so hard that the grave could not be dug. In those instances, the body was placed in the barn on the laying-out board until the ground thawed sufficiently for burial to proceed. Flowers were not a part of the wake or burial ceremony traditionally in Appalachia.

Death unified the mountain community in a way few other events could. Men joined together to build the casket and as many as twelve at a time took up shovels to dig the grave. As with the abundant food gifts, no payment was ever asked for these community services. It was just the way neighbors treated each other back then. Every family that helped knew that, sooner or later, they would also have a need for help from the members of their community.

In preparation for the wake, a casket was built from whatever wood was readily available. Chestnut, pine, oak, and poplar were usually the chosen woods in the mountains of West Virginia. Some mountaineers had their coffins already built and leaning up against a wall in the barn! The first settlers in West Virginia were buried in tree trunks or "tree coffins." A section of tree approximately as long as the deceased person was cut and hollowed out. Once the body was placed inside the trunk, the top of the log was put back on and the body was ready for burial. Later, crude coffins were fashioned and painted black to hide the rough-hewn finish. Cotton batting served to pad these coffins and white cotton or some other fabric was placed inside as a lining. Eventually, coffins were crafted with more skill and craftsmanship with handles from the general store and the pine, oak, poplar, or chestnut wood of the casket was finished with more dexterity.

Superstitions Surrounding the Dead

The Appalachian Mountains are full of superstitions surrounding death. These superstitions are carefully followed although most folks cannot say how or why they believe in their efficacy. If the deceased person's eyes are left open, they were looking to find someone to take with them. A dead body must be carried feet first or the soul will return to haunt the family. Another common belief was that leaving a funeral before it was over will bring bad luck upon you and everyone knew that a pregnant woman should never attend a funeral. Concerning the gravesite itself, an open grave should never be left overnight. Water in an open grave means the person buried there will be restless and walk about after death. It was widely believed that no grass would grow on the grave of an evil person. It is still believed that if someone plants a cedar, he will die when it grows tall enough to shade his grave.

Preparation of the home where the wake is held must be made carefully according to Appalachian tradition. First, all clocks must be stopped and all mirrors covered and turned to the wall. It was believed that the next person to look into a mirror after a death occurred would die. Then, all doors must be unlocked and all windows opened so the deceased will be able to move on and make the transition into the next world. A gust of wind may enter the room once you have opened all the windows. It has come to carry the deceased person's soul away. Never leave a rocking chair rocking or you will be inviting death. My grandmother carefully reached back and stopped the rocking chair from moving after she stood up and I never realized why until I grew up and started researching the old ways.

When it is time to remove the body from the home, take care to carry it out feet first or it will return to haunt the family. Make sure you touch the deceased at some point during the wake to prevent the soul of that person from haunting you. Never wear anything new to a funeral and be especially careful to wear old shoes.

Bodies were traditionally buried facing east to be ready for Judgment Day when the angels would arrive from that direction to sound their trumpets. However, if the consensus of the community was that the dead person was unrighteous, the body would be buried the opposite direction, facing west. Those who committed suicide were greatly feared because the living thought they would return to haunt them. Therefore, suicides and anyone dying outside the covering of righteous living, were often buried at a crossroads (symbolizing the cross of Jesus) since they were not permitted burial on sacred land.

An old wake custom that is still practiced in some parts of the mountains is called "saining"- usually performed by one of the older women in the family. Saining involves lighting a candle and waving it three times over the corpse. Then three handfuls of salt would be placed in a wooden bowl on the deceased person's chest. This ritual was necessary to keep the corpse from sitting up in the coffin due to rigor mortis. Even after the widespread practice of embalming, there are still a few folks who practice this ritual.

Sin Eaters

We cannot leave the topic of death in the mountains without a quick mention of the practice of sin-eating. A sin eater is a person who assumes the sins of the deceased by eating or drinking as part of the ritual of absolution. This form of scapegoating can trace its roots back to the Jewish Day of Atonement rituals (Yom Kippur) in which a goat ritually assumes the sins of an entire village before being driven off into the wilderness. Along with many other ideas and customs, the practice of sin eating in Appalachian society was brought over from the British Isles where the practice was common in Scotland, England, and Wales.

The sin eater was thought to be eternally damned as a result of absorbing the sin stains of the dead and dying, but during his or her lifetime, enjoyed the attention of the community, the consolation of a life of public service, a small fee, and some free meals. Of course, a stranger passing through the community would make the perfect sin-eater as he would soon leave the area taking with him the sins of the deceased. If a stranger could not be found and convinced to participate, the resident sin eater would be called upon for his services.

Upon arrival at the dying person's bedside, the sin eater would recite a ritualistic prayer, eat the bread or other food placed on the dying person's chest, and receive a cup of beverage passed to him over the body. The actual eating and imbibing of the food and drink were symbolic of taking the sins of the person upon himself to bear on Judgment Day. The Roman Catholic Church considers sin eating a cardinal sin as they believe only a priest can offer the sacrament of absolution from sin. Most Protestant faiths believe that Jesus Christ has already provided the route to forgiveness and absolution of sin through acceptance of his sacrifice upon the cross so they also do not look favorably upon the practice. However, sin eating is still practiced in remote areas in Appalachia as well as in Wales and a few other locations and was a common practice in most European countries at one time.

The actual ritual of sin-eating is said to begin with a cup of water, a spoonful of salt, and a piece of bread that is placed on the bare chest of the deceased. The sin-eater takes a pinch of salt and adds it to the water and then takes the cup of water in his right hand. Before drinking the salty water, the sin-eater intones, "With this salted water that has rested on your corpse, (name of deceased), I now drink away all the sins that are upon you. May they pass from your body into mine." The sin-eater would then pass the cup of water counterclockwise over the head of the deceased three times drinking a mouthful and pouring out the rest through the fingers of his left hand. The procedure and incantation is repeated using the bread that was also placed on the bare chest of the dead body. The sin-eater then crumbled the remainder of the bread, dropped it onto the floor, and stepped on it.

How does one become a sin-eater? As a civil servant performing a public service, in some areas the sin eater is chosen by vote or even by public lot. I have heard about a few occasions where a traveler or unsuspecting stranger was asked to perform this service when no one else was available. Although every village of old required a sin eater to remove the deceased person's sin so he or she would not return to haunt the village, the general public shunned the sin eater and steered clear of him. He had to forego the pleasures of taking a wife. Nor could he enjoy the other comforts of civilization. Often he was only permitted to come into the public's eye when he had a duty to perform; otherwise he was made to live as a leper on the outskirts of the village.

A Mountain Woman' Goodbye

     Although death is accepted with a fatalistic and almost business-like matter-of-factness, we cannot end this chapter without reflecting on the reason why this might be so. To help you understand the calm acceptance of a loved one's passing, I must introduce you to a dear lady in Webster County, West Virginia, who writes beautiful poetry from her heart. Her name is Bertie Jane Cutlip but she calls herself the "Apple Butter, Jelly, Pepper Relish, Poetry Woman." Mike and I met her one May at the annual Webster Springs Wildflower Hike at Camp Caesar in Cowan. Bertie Jane's tiny, smiling face belies the fact that life has not been easy or altogether kind. She writes poetry and cans jellies and relishes to sell and augment her slender income. She captured our hearts at a poetry reading one night as she recited several poems from heart. The following simple poem captures the essence of the mountain dweller's faith in God and the joyful hope and belief that family and friends can look forward to a future great reunion when a loved one passes. Perhaps the thoughts expressed in Bertie Jane's simple poem explain this idea best of all.

A Friends' Daughter

We miss you so our Bonnie Sue
Since God took you away
Although it's been eight long years
We think of you each day.

It's hard for us to understand
The grief we have to bear
So we'll just live the best we can
And try to meet you over there.

The next chapter – Visits To (and From) the Dead – tells of how the living and the dead visit each other in the mountains of West Virginia. The practice of eating on the grounds on Memorial Day is described and still practiced in areas of Appalachia. This chapter also includes stories about encounters with the dead that are true but never told or published before. Some of these happenings were related to me by family members and other stories were told by strangers. The true story of how a ghost's testimony convicted a local man of murder rounds out this chapter on visits to (and from) the dead.

Chapter 5

Visits To (And From) the Dead

In Appalachian folk culture, the dead are always very near the living. This chapter will show you some of the ways that this interaction has traditionally occurred in West Virginia. As you will soon see, sometimes the living seek out the dead and sometimes it happens the other way! First, we will examine the custom of eating on the grounds – a virtual family reunion of the living and the dead, complete with picnic tables in the graveyard. Then we will hear some true stories of the dead walking among us. The final pages of this chapter will relate the well-known and often-told true story of how a ghost's testimony convicted a West Virginia man of murder.

Eating on the Grounds Appalachian Tradition

Every year on Decoration Day, or Memorial Day, mini-pilgrimages occur throughout the state of West Virginia and the other states included in the region called Southern Appalachia. Family members travel – sometimes only a matter of miles and sometimes literally days – to converge on their family cemeteries for a custom that is found only in Southern Appalachia. In the Duffield Family Cemetery in Duck as well as in many others scattered across Southern Appalachia, this practice referred to as "eating on the grounds" still takes place on Decoration

Day, or Memorial Day, every year. Some folks refer to this practice as a "homecoming"- an annual gathering between May and November that is held in a cemetery. Dr. Karen Li Simpkins says, "The Homecomings are part and parcel of the old Communion Season; the May-November seasonal round of congregational and family reunions held in many evangelical tradition Protestant cultures."

The tradition of eating on the grounds began in Southern Appalachia in small, isolated, rural cemeteries where the families involved would gather to pay their respects to the deceased and to maintain the cemetery. Then, as now, most family homecomings or "eating on the grounds" activities begin with Memorial Day, or Decoration Day, celebrations. First, all the graves are cleaned of debris, sticks, trash and dilapidated decorations. Decades ago, the graves were freshly scraped and all grass and vegetation was removed from the gravesites. Today, the graves are generally grass-covered and freshly mowed. After World War II, plastic flowers replaced many of the fresh, paper, or waxed floral arrangements previously used to mark each grave. More recently, most folks have replaced plastic with silk floral arrangements – some simple and others incredibly elaborate and expensive. Occasionally, you will also find the graves of war veterans marked with small American flags.

Most of these cemetery homecomings, or eating on the grounds ceremonies, occur off the beaten path at small family cemeteries located up back roads and country lanes. After the maintenance of the graveyard is finished, a traditional meal is served in the cemetery. This meal serves as a family reunion of sorts where families can not only maintain the family cemetery, but also visit and remember those who had gone on to their reward.

Cultural geographer D. Gregory Jeane refers to this practice of graveyard maintenance workdays as part of the cult of piety and states these workdays and dinners traditionally occurred in late summer or early fall. Today, the cemetery upkeep and dinner on the grounds usually starts with Decoration Day in May, with some families holding subsequent events throughout the summer and fall. Folk studies scholar, Lynwood Montell, informs us that cemetery cleanings are a form of group or family ritual behavior accompanied by a communal sharing of food. He mentions that the events that take place on Decoration Day in the graveyards of Southern Appalachia are as much for the living as for the dead. Jeane says that cemetery cleanings not only serve as a means of sustaining and upholding the physical appearance of the cemetery, but also comprise a social gathering for the local area or as a family reunion that brings relatives together again.

In West Virginia, Kentucky, and much of Southern Appalachia, families still meet at their traditional family cemetery on Decoration Day. They spend the day cleaning and decorating the graves with new silk floral arrangements and visiting while they eat delicious picnic foods. This holiday serves a two-fold purpose – a time of remembering family members who no longer are with us and a time of reconnecting with family members still among the living. Journalist Georgia Stamper calls this time "a spontaneous reunion among the tombstones." She muses "to those from the city, or from the north, I suppose a cemetery might sound like an odd setting for a jolly get-together, but it seemed appropriate to me then – and still does now. I always thought the dead could hear our talk and our laughter, and were as kindly disposed to our bringing a party to them as for bringing the memorial flowers."

Writer Charlotte Deskins remembers how her family in McDowell County would converge on the Collins family cemetery in late August for a three-day "dinner on the ground." This happy reunion of those living and those no longer alive took place in the family cemetery and was accompanied by preaching, singing, lots of talk and gossip, eating country food in abundance, horse-trading, and matchmaking! Her relatives relate that during the 1940's and 1950's, everyone spread clean sheets on the ground in the cemetery and actually dined on the ground picnic-style. Later, family members constructed sturdy tables that now serve to hold the baskets and bowls of delicious country cooking.

I was introduced to this custom by my husband, Michael. When we married in the 1970's, he told me about how his family always had a get-together in the Duffield Family Cemetery in Clay County on Memorial Day. Having been raised up north in Pennsylvania, I had a hard time understanding and relating to this practice. My family rarely visited the graves of our deceased family members and certainly would not even consider the practice of picnicking among the graves! The most we did was plant some marigolds on the graves of immediate family members and attend the local VFW parade and ceremony held annually at the cemetery on Memorial Day. The first time Michael asked me to pack a picnic lunch and go with him to his distant and remote family graveyard, I was sure he was crazy! However, I baked a cake and threw together some cold cuts and bread and off we went to join the rest of his family at the Duffield Family Cemetery in Clay County.

The Duffield Family Cemetery is high on a hilltop surrounded by mountains and fertile grassy valleys. I have never been in a more peaceful or beautiful part of West Virginia than this remote rural setting. The cemetery was once part of a family farm back in the times when deceased family members were laid out in the family home and then buried in the family graveyard. Not just a family graveyard, the John M. Duffield Memorial Cemetery is the final home of members of several local families. Charles William Duffield originally owned the land the cemetery lies on. His son, John McHenry Duffield donated the land for the cemetery and John's daughter, three-year old

Martha Duffield, was the first person to be buried there on November 15, 1870 (from the gravestone).

The graves in this cemetery reflect the patterns of kinship and intermarriage that have occurred for generations in West Virginia between rural families within limited spatial areas. The cemetery is named for John McHenry Duffield but many other area families are represented here as well. Argabrite, Duffield, Gillespie, Greathouse, Hayes, Howe, McLaughlin, McMorrow, Mollohan, Nichols, Nottingham, Pettit, Sears, Sirk, Spencer, White, and Wiseman are just some of the surnames found on the gravestones here. Upon investigation, one will notice that several of the family names are interrelated — mute evidence of the links between families in this region. Susan Edna Sirk Duffield and Bessie Duffield Gillespie Vandergrift are two women who have served as links between families through intermarriage. Violet Wheeler, mother of Genevieve (Jean) Wheeler Gillespie, my husband's mother, came the greatest distance to rest here. She lived her entire life in Brooklyn, New York, and came to live with her daughter Jean's family in Parkersburg when she became ill.

The cemetery is not easily accessed and, once off the paved road, the trip is not for the faint-of-heart. First, you must drive up a steep, dirt road negotiating sharp drop-offs on one side while avoiding a deep ditch on the other. On one occasion my husband drove too close to the edge of the road and the right side wheels literally dropped-off the road. We had a few anxious moments as we all scrambled out of the vehicle and had another family member, his cousin, Adrian, pull us out of harm's way and back onto the road! The road used to be all but impassable during the rainy season unless one had a four-wheel drive vehicle. Today it is in much better condition and not as treacherous.

When I first started coming to the graveyard, there was a rickety wooden fence around the graveyard and cows were always escaping their pasture and gaining access to the hallowed ground through a gate carelessly left ajar or a broken fence. Several years ago however, the caretaker family passed the hat and enough money was raised to surround the graveyard with a sturdy fence and gate ensuring that cows and their unwanted friends – flies – were not a problem.

    My husband remembers how his family would drive 70 miles of winding two-lane backroads to spend Decoration Day at the Duffield Family Cemetery when he was a child. His mother, Jean Gillespie, would always tell him to stay clean but that was not always possible in a mountaintop graveyard surrounded by cow pasture! He and his brother and cousins would run around playing ball and deviling his little sister, Lynn. Michael said the adults would dress in church clothes with the men in white shirts and the women in print dresses for these special get-togethers on Decoration Day. He said he and his siblings always looked forward to seeing their cousins and eating the tasty selection of wholesome country foods.

    Diane Duffield Nottingham, Michael's second-cousin, grew-up on the farm adjoining the family cemetery. Her family has been involved with the graveyard's maintenance for many years. Diane's father, Jack Duffield, renovated the cemetery in the 1950's by re-marking many of the graves and leveling out the traditionally-mounded graves for easier mowing and upkeep. Now, family members living nearby maintain the cemetery with the help of monetary contributions from family living at a distance.

    Diane recently reminisced with us about the tables full of fried chicken, homemade noodles, potato salad, meat loaf, fresh-baked bread, and pies and cakes of every kind and description. The favorite dessert was always warm, moist apple cake, Diane said, and cheese and squash casserole was always a big hit along with deviled eggs and green beans. She told me that before picnic tables were built in the cemetery, everyone spread blankets out on the grass and literally dined on the ground! The women had cooked all week to have enough food for the many family members who traveled to the cemetery – some from great distances. If a preacher was handy, he would bless the food and everyone would eat and visit, catching up on family news and gossip. She remembered that a Mormon preacher and a Christian Adventist minister both were in attendance in the graveyard on Decoration Day but doesn't recall either of them preaching a service there. They did, however, bless the food before everyone began to eat.

Diane shared with me that everyone knew by word-of-mouth when the Decoration Day event was scheduled to take place. Back in the 1940's and 1950's, it was an organized event in the community. Diane remembers her mother and aunts would spend a great deal of time arranging live flowers in containers that they would place on every grave in the Duffield Cemetery. At that time, Diane recalls the cemetery contained over 30 graves. Today, silk floral arrangements have taken the place of live flowers on most of the graves. The graves, as is common in Southern Appalachian family cemeteries, have an eastern orientation so that when Judgment Day arrives and "the last trumpet is sounded, the dead in Christ shall rise" facing Jerusalem. Even the youngest children are taught not to sit on the tombstones or walk on the graves but instead, to respectfully walk around them.

This "eating on the grounds" or "dinner on the grounds" custom is linked to religious church homecomings but there are differences. The church-related cemeteries are situated next to churches and always have a preaching service along with the outdoor dinner on the grounds as part of the church's annual homecoming celebration. However, many of the older West Virginia family cemeteries have never been connected to a particular church and now are regularly visited by families on

Memorial Day without a religious service or even the presence of a preacher.

    My husband's family has continued the custom of eating on the grounds on Decoration Day although it is a more subdued low-key affair than he remembers from the days of his childhood in the 1950's. Today we gather at the Duffield Family Cemetery and eat out of coolers since the old wooden picnic tables are long gone. We sit in folding lawn chairs and set up two or three folding aluminum tables to hold the platters and bowls of food. Fried chicken, meat and cheese sandwiches, pickles, potato salad, chips, and cookies make up the menu for our eating on the grounds lunch. There is always a chocolate birthday cake to celebrate Aunt Pauline's birthday and plenty of cookies and candy since the Gillespie clan is known for our sweet tooth.

    Today you are likely to catch us in shorts and sandals instead of our Sunday church clothes, reflective, I think, of today's more casual lifestyle. But everything else is the same as it's always been for over a century. We still eat heartily and leisurely while trading family news and thumbing through envelopes of photographs. Some folks bring family photo albums and talk invariably drifts to plans for the next official Gillespie family reunion. It seems we cannot properly enjoy our get-togethers without planning with relish and great anticipation the next one! Older family members shake hands and greet visitors to the graveyard because they inevitably know someone in their family. Community gossip and family news updates are exchanged with the newcomers and they are always invited to grab a plate and sit down.

    Fresh silk floral arrangements are placed on the graves of family members and noses are blown and tears shed because memories are strong and powerful up there on the hill. Tears and laughter mix and mingle in this hilltop piece of heaven. A beautiful gravestone of black granite marks the final resting place of our young nephew, Mathew

Gillespie, who died suddenly and unexpectedly when only 15 years of age. A beautiful laser-etched image of Mathew winding up to pitch in his baseball uniform is an eternal tribute to the special young man we all remember and love. We also pause at Violet Wheeler's grave. She was my husband's beautiful grandmother from Brooklyn, New York. She certainly came the farthest to attend this family reunion. Then cameras come out as each family wants mementoes to commemorate this very important annual family event. This is a yearly mini-family reunion of sorts and Gillespie family members come from as far away as South Carolina and Indiana to participate. There is no need to rush the eating or the visiting and we surely do not.

This cemetery serves as a miniature map of the community – a community that still reveres its agrarian roots - a community that continues to value family, friends, and faith in God. As Bobbie Ann Mason, award-winning Appalachian author, in her autobiography *Clear Springs*, said as she stood in her old family cemetery in Kentucky, "But our history was mapped out here in Clear Springs, like the fencerows edging the fields that spread out in all directions. The history seemed to rise from the land wrapping around me." So it is with the Duffield Cemetery. The history of many local families is told by reading the gravestones and listening to the stories and reminiscences of folks who gather on Decoration Day every year to decorate the graves and enjoy a family picnic in the cemetery.

One true story that has always caused children to listen open-mouthed is the story of the double murder of Draper Camden (Cam) Duffield and his son, Corbett Duffield that occurred while they were digging a family member's grave here in 1921. Harry Duffield, Jr. told this story to me in 2006 as his father related it to him. Harry's grandfather, Hardy Duffield, was a witness to this double murder and has passed down the facts I am about to relate to you.

This father and son were shot and killed by Cam's nephews, Orville and Freeman Duffield, in a dispute over a horse-drawn sled. This long-standing family feud had been stewing for many years in the Duffield family. Two young teenage brothers, Orville and Freeman Duffield, had stolen a horse-drawn sled from a woman. She pressed charges and a trial was held on Harold Duffield's front porch (this story is told by Harold Duffield in "Hickory and Ladyslippers- A History of Clay County.)" Uncle Cam Duffield was a witness against the two brothers so he testified against them. Needless to say, the guilty verdict caused great anger among some of the bystanders and a huge fight broke out involving several family members. Uncle Cam got beat up trying to stop the fistfight. His son, Corbett was not at the trial but was greatly angered because his father had been beaten. Whenever he saw the teenagers in the community he told them he was going to lick them for beating up his father.

The feud reached a fever-pitch one sultry day in early July 1921. The day of the double murders, several members of the community were at the cemetery preparing a grave for a little Hodge girl who had just died. Cam and Corbett were digging the grave under a large tree in the cemetery (the tree is still standing today). Orville and Freeman Duffield, reputed to be feisty and always eager for a fight, entered the cemetery and challenged Uncle Cam and Corbett to a fistfight. When Uncle Cam refused, Orville took out a Colt 32 automatic pistol and shot him as he stood in the grave. Then he shot Corbett who was standing on the ground near the grave and he toppled into the hole, too. The story as told by Harold Duffield in "Hickory and Ladyslippers- A History of Clay County" and included in Hilda Sirk Pettit's "Times Twisted Trail," tells a slightly different tale from here. It says that Corbett met the brothers at the gate of the cemetery where he informed them he planned to whip them for beating up his father. Orville pulled out a gun and threatened Corbett with it, but it was Freeman who took the gun and shot Corbett three times, killing him instantly. Uncle Cam ran out to the gate as Corbett was falling and was shot twice. The brothers just walked away and were later placed in the jail in Clay County. A few days later the boys broke out of jail and the largest manhunt ever staged in Clay County began. Volunteers were deputized, law enforcement officers from nearby counties joined, and bloodhounds were used to track the brothers down. After several days, Orville and Freeman were caught, tried, and both sentenced to life in prison in the largest murder trial ever held in Clay County. Orville got an early release, broke parole, and re-entered prison for a period of time. When he was released again, he lived a quiet life in Ivydale until he passed on. Freeman went straight upon his release from prison. The old oak tree under which they were probably murdered still stands in the middle of the graveyard.

Family members share stories about the deceased as if it was just yesterday that they were living and breathing. When the talk slows and we are drowsy from the food and the warmth of the sun, we simply gaze out over the valleys and treetops and I know the same question crosses each of our minds – "who will be the next one to join our growing family on the hill?"

As the afternoon sun starts to slant and the shadows lengthen, we pack up our vehicles and drive to the Westfall family cemetery in Braxton County. This pilgrimage involves crossing a creek and traversing yet another steep and winding road. This tiny family burial ground contains older graves and reflects the earlier Gillespie ancestors. Many of the gravestones have fallen over or shifted out of place. The deep forest seems to threaten to swallow this graveyard up and small animals rustling in the underbrush always give me an eerie feeling. Someone always comments on the number of graves that had to be dug one winter when a particularly virulent outbreak of influenza claimed entire families. Occasionally we run into old friends and family members at this location and break out the food again for one last feast before we pack up and head for home. A few years ago on Memorial Day we encountered two brothers hand-digging a grave in this cemetery. These gravediggers have worked together hand-digging graves for decades and buried many of the dead in the county over the years. Watching them dig the graves was a lesson in cooperation and symmetry. They worked harmoniously together without breaking rhythm even while they talked with us.

After attending my husband's Memorial Day "eating on the grounds" events for 30 years, I can honestly say that, sadness for the dead aside, you come away from these get-togethers closer and tighter-knit as a family. Distant kin may not see you for another year, but as long as your name is not on a new headstone or temporary grave marker, they know they will see you again in May. Lately, various Appalachian scholars claim this tradition of "eating on the grounds" is no longer a part of the culture of rural West Virginia. They say the tradition has disappeared and families no longer take part in Decoration Day "eating on the grounds." However, I respectfully must disagree. I have been to many such celebrations of family in my husband's rural West Virginia family graveyards and will continue to attend until it's my turn to take my place permanently with the family "up on the hill."

Visits FROM the Dead!

Sometimes we don't need to visit the dead – they come to find us! After perusing dozens of true tales of ghostly visits to the living, I have come to the conclusion that most of these visits are made to benefit, and not harm or threaten, the living. Strangely enough this next true story also involves Memorial Day but this time the dead made the first move!

In Pendleton County, on an early Memorial Day morning, Dean and Marie Morgan were taking the scenic and picturesque narrow mountain road that led to Franklin. This was their first time visiting the region and they were very excited that their friends had invited them to their home in Franklin for the day. The mountain vistas were breathtaking and the air fresh and clean!

They were almost to a bridge that crossed a deep mountain gorge when Marie noticed a small child standing beside the road. She asked her husband to stop so they could help the little girl. Right away the couple was struck by the child's odd appearance. Her clothing was out-of-date and her long brown hair was parted and secured on each side with large ribbon bows. The little one had a pale, thin face and dark sunken eyes and they thought she was ill and had wandered away from her family and lost her way.

Dean asked if they could help her in any way. The little girl replied she had a bouquet of flowers that she wanted to place on a grave in the cemetery just up the road. She said she would certainly appreciate a ride if they were going that way. Dean opened the back car door and the little girl climbed in.

On the way, she told the couple that her name was Miriam and she was visiting her mother's grave to put the bouquet on it in memory of her departed mother. She looked so sad and unhappy that Dean and Marie soon stopped asking questions and let her rest in the back seat.

Soon they saw the church graveyard up ahead. Marie turned around to ask the child if this was the cemetery she wanted to visit. To her great surprise and concern, the little girl was gone! Dean jumped out checked the back door but found it still locked relieving them that she had not fallen out of the vehicle, at least. But where was she? They both ran around the car looking back down the road they had just come up in dismay.

Just then, they noticed a woman in the cemetery waving at them and "yoo-hooing." As the Morgans entered the cemetery, the woman asked if there was anything wrong. They seemed so upset to her.

Marie and Dean explained the little girl's abrupt disappearance from their car and expressed concern for her safety. The woman asked if the child had told them her name.

"Why, yes, she did," Marie said. "Her name is Miriam Thomas. She told us she was taking some flowers to place on her mother's grave."

"Well, Miriam was my sister. She and mother died in a horse and buggy accident ten years ago when Miriam was only ten years old. You met her near the bridge, didn't you?"

"Yes, we saw her there by the side of the road near the bridge."

"Mother lost control of the horse when it balked at crossing the bridge. The buggy wrecked and both mother and Miriam were thrown into the water. Mother's body was recovered but they never found Miriam. But every year on Memorial Day, Miriam brings flowers for mother's grave. See, there they are already! I must have been in the church when she came so I missed her."

Marie and Dean could only stare at the lovely bouquet of fresh spring flowers on the grave the woman pointed out. They carefully made their way back to their car and drove the rest of the way to Franklin in shock. It was many years before they were able to share this true story.

Brooke County Visit from Beyond the Grave

Another true story about the dead coming to find us takes place in Colliers, Brooke County in the 1930's. Now everyone in the world knows that Colliers claim to fame is that it was the site of the first bare knuckle world heavyweight championship on June 1, 1880! But read on and hear the story one Colliers resident remembers her grandfather relating to her many times throughout her childhood.

This story starts with the teller's great-grandfather who moved to Colliers. A few weeks after his move, he was sitting on is back porch of his rented house enjoying the cool evening, when he noticed an old man walking down the railroad tracks. This was not unusual because hobos were always jumping trains.

The great-grandfather watched as the old man kept lifting a bottle to his lips and taking a hearty swig. He sat down on the railroad tracks and kept drinking until the great-grandfather became concerned. The old man would be too drunk to get off the tracks and the 9:15 freight train was due in five minutes! By this time the great-grandmother had joined her husband on the back porch. She, too, became upset about the old hobo's impending fate.

Finally, the great-grandfather jumped off the porch and took off running the quarter-mile to the tracks to help the hobo. He heard the coming train's warning whistle but couldn't push himself any harder. He started yelling to the hobo to wake up and get off the tracks. The old hobo didn't move or even appear to hear him shouting!

The great-grandfather gave up. He was about to witness a horrible death because the fast-moving train could not slow down, or even stop, and the hobo was still on the tracks. But, right before his very eyes, as the engine started to hit the hobo – the old drunken hobo vanished into thin air!

The great-grandfather could not believe what he just saw! He searched the tracks and the bushes around them thoroughly, convinced he had seen the old hobo with his bottle. He walked back to his house and told his wife, who also had seen the hobo on the tracks. She could only shake her head in disbelief, too, as he recounted what he had seen.

This incident troubled the couple so much that they finally went to their landlord with their story. Convinced he would think they were crazy, they told him what they had seen and experienced. The landlord did not think they were insane. In fact, he made them sit down and told them the story of the old hobo.

Many years ago, an old man arrived in Colliers. The locals did not exactly roll out the welcome mat for him as they were leery of strangers who arrived without bag and baggage. When the stranger finally got drunk, the locals ran him off. Dejected, the old man sat on the railroad tracks to wait for the next train to arrive. When the train came, it killed the old man.

Ever since that time, on the anniversary of the old man's death, he returns and waits for the train. No one could pass by that stretch of tracks, however, without their horse balking and refusing to go near. The teller's great-grandfather was the only person to ever get near the scene of the accident. He tried to help the old hobo and perhaps, that was why he was allowed to get so close.

The following year, on the anniversary of this strange death, the great-grandfather waited to see the hobo reappear on the tracks at precisely 9:15 again. But – he never appeared. The train came and went with nothing out-of-the-ordinary occurring. The old man on the railroad never reappeared again after that. Some of the more religious town folk say that the old drunk hobo's ghost finally received what he was looking for – a helping hand from someone who wanted to do a good deed to his fellow man!

Wirt County Lady in White

    This true story still brings chills on a hot summer day to members of my family! Very few people have ever heard it told because my father-in-law, Bill Gillespie, was a man of few words and went to his grave doubting what he saw that day with his very own eyes. The story he told begins on a warm October day in 1980 when he and my husband, Mike, were squirrel hunting in the Oxbow area of Wirt County. The sun was shining and neither man had bagged their limit. After a quick sandwich in their vehicle, father and son split up and went their separate ways to continue the hunt.

    As Mike headed off down the old road, Bill decided to head over the ridge to a location full of beech and hickory trees. As he crested the ridge top and started down the hill, he noticed an old house sitting in the bottomland below. The house had not been painted for a long time and the grey boards shined silvery in the warm autumn sun. Since the house looked deserted, Bill thought he would take a few minutes and poke around in the weeds for old bottles, which he liked to collect. He proceeded down the hill, looking for snakes underfoot and dodging the thorn bushes.

    As he approached the house, he noticed a woman in one of the downstairs windows. She was waving at him and motioning him to come inside. Bill remembers she had on a white dress and long hair flowing around her shoulders. He went up on the porch and thought he would go inside to see if she needed some help since she had so vigorously motioned for him to enter the house. He opened the old door hesitantly since vines had crept up and tangled around the doorknob and entranceway. Once inside, he walked into the room where the woman had been and saw....... nothing! He called for her to no avail.

But that wasn't the scary part. Bill looked at the floor directly beside the window where the woman had been standing. The boards were missing and a gaping hole in the floor made it impossible for a person to stand at the window! Even though Bill admitted he has never believed in ghosts, apparitions, or spirits of any kind that did not come from a bottle, he lost no time in running from that old house. When his son returned to the vehicle, he saw his father already sitting in the front seat waiting for him. Mike thought his Dad was having a heart attack because he looked so pale. To my knowledge, Bill never told this story to anyone outside the immediate family. When my husband offered to go back and check the house out for the woman, Bill refused to even give him its location. My husband, too, is reluctant to try and find it but I know the woman in white is there and probably still waiting for some company!

This Ghostly Visitation Brought Justice!

One of the best-documented true stories of ghostly visits from the dead is actually recorded in the Lewisburg courthouse in Greenbrier County. Not only are there court records, but also a road sign that attests to the fact that the ghost of Zona Heaster Shue helped convict her murderer of his heinous crime.

The story begins back in 1886 when a man called Edward S. Shue lived on Rock Camp Run, Pocahontas County, with his first wife. Shue was a handsome, well-built man but had the vile habit of beating his wife. It was no surprise to the neighbors, therefore, when she divorced him while he was serving time in the state penitentiary for horse theft.

Shue lost no time in finding another wife when he was released from prison. His handsome good looks and virile masculinity soon captured the attention of another young woman and she became his second wife. They lived on top of Droop Mountain in Pocahontas County. Unfortunately, his second wife died suddenly of mysterious causes. Shue once again found himself in the market for a wife.

The story takes off on two roads now. What we know for certain is that Edward Shue met and married a pretty young fifteen-year-old girl named Zona Heaster. They were married in Greenbrier County in the United Methodist Church at Livesay's Mill in November 1896. Some folks say Zona was lured to Droop Mountain to visit her uncle and while there, was convinced to marry Shue. Others say she took one look at his strong, virile physique and fell madly in love with him. Whatever course the meeting and courtship took, the end result was clear. Against her parent's wishes, Zona Heaster married Edward Shue and became Wife #3!

Zona set up housekeeping with Edward in a two-story frame building in Livesay's Mill where Shue worked as a blacksmith for James Crookshanks. Two months after the marriage, in January 1987, Zona fell ill and was cared for by Dr. J.M. Knapp for several weeks. On the morning of January 22, Shue went to the cabin of "Aunt" Martha Jones, a Negro woman of good report in the community. He requested her 11-year-old son, Anderson Jones, come to his house and do some chores and cleaning for Mrs. Shue. Because Anderson was already doing tasks for Dr. Knapp, he was not free to come immediately and history tells us that Shue returned four times to see if Anderson was free to come yet.

It was close to 1:00 PM when Anderson finally knocked on the Shue's kitchen door. Unable to raise anyone, he walked into the kitchen and from there entered the dining room. Stumbling over something, he looked down and let out a scream heard in the next county. Mrs. Shue's body lay, eyes wide open and unseeing, before him on the dining room floor! Anderson ran to get Dr. Knapp who came immediately.

When he arrived, he found Shue embracing his wife and crying for her to come back. Shue had placed Zona on her bed and put an old-fashioned stiff high collar and scarf around her neck. Dr. Knapp tried to determine if Zona was still alive but Edward did not permit the doctor to get near her head for some reason. Dr. Knapp finally declared Zona's death was due to a heart attack.

The next day, Zona's body was returned for burial to her family graveyard on the other side of the mountain. Another account says she was buried in the churchyard of Soule Chapel Church in Greenbrier County. Regardless of where Zona's final resting place lay, something rather strange occurred before she was buried. Observant folks wondered and commented on Shue's devotion to his dead young wife. He absolutely refused to leave her side and stood at the head of her casket the entire time until she was buried. Others wondered at the way Shue had placed a rolled-up sheet on one side of her head and another piece of clothing near the other side – as if to balance her head and hold it upright.

One would think the sad story should end here. Three young wives – two of who died early, tragic deaths. A grief-stricken husband in mourning once again. But no! Here is the interesting part and the reason this story is included in this chapter on visits to (and from) the dead in the first place!

Zona's aging mother, Mrs. Heaster, was very upset and fairly suspicious about her daughter's sudden death. She had always been a devoutly religious woman all her life, so she prayed constantly and begged the good Lord to reveal to her the true cause of her daughter's death. Several days after her daughter's funeral, Mrs. Heaster was awakened in the middle of the night by a noise. Looking about her room she was startled to see Zona standing there in the dress she wore at her funeral! As Mrs. Heaster reached out to touch her daughter, Zona disappeared.

However, during the next four nights, Her daughter reappeared in her bedroom and informed Mrs. Heaster of how the crime was committed. These ghostly visitations from her dead daughter convinced her that Shue had murdered Zona in cold blood. But how could she convince the authorities? She had no evidence or proof.

Mrs. Heaster found an ally in Prosecuting Attorney John A. Preston who believed her story after talking with her. Dr. Knapp was questioned as to the cause of Zona's death and admitted that she had not died from a heart attack. Preston ordered several neighbors to exhume Zona's grave. It was only after he had repeatedly threatened arrest that the men finally disinterred Zona's remains from her grave. After all, graves were always closed in Greenbrier County – never opened!

Dr. Knapp examined the corpse, working feverishly for three days and nights until he determined the true cause of Zona's death. Zona had died of a broken neck! She had prepared her husband's supper that night in January. When he came home, he discovered she had prepared applesauce, bread, jellies, and other tasty items but no meat! Edward flew into a hot-tempered rage and seized her head and twisted it, dislocating her neck and killing her. He cleverly covered this fact up with the high collar and rolled-up sheets in the coffin.

The autopsy provided enough evidence to arrest and charge Edward Shue with murder. The trial began in the Lewisburg Circuit Court on June 30, 1897. When Mrs. Heaster testified during the trial about Zona's ghostly nocturnal visits, her evidence was so compelling that the editor of the *Greenbrier Independent,* Thomas H. Dennis, printed her entire testimony from start to finish - something never done before! Mrs. Heaster insisted she was wide awake during each of her daughter's ghostly visitations and that she was not dreaming. She even admitted to having touched Zona's arm once and said she found it solid although cold as ice.

The jury found Edward Shue guilty of murder, and he was sentenced to life in prison. Some of the locals tried to lynch Shue, reasoning that he should die from a broken neck as his wife had done. Having survived the lynching attempt, Shue was sent to Moundsville Penitentiary where he died eight years later. *Case's Comment*, a national lawyer's magazine, claims that the murder of Zona Heaster Shue is the only case in the United States where a man has been convicted of murder on the testimony of a ghost. Zona's story is one of West Virginia's premier ghostly tales and she is often referred to as the Greenbrier Ghost.

The final chapter of this book tells the strange legend of Strange Creek and how it received its name. The story of Booger Hole, a legendary hamlet that once breathed hellfire and brimstone, is also recounted. The finishing story of this book recounts the story of the Ritchie Mines, a legendary liquid asphalt mine that once flourished in the hollows near Macfarlan in Ritchie County, West Virginia. Sit back, re-fill that coffee cup or sweet tea glass, and enjoy the final tales of some strange and wonderful locations here in the Appalachian hills and hollows of West Virginia!

Chapter 6

Strange Creek, Booger Hole, and
The Mine that Paved the Streets of Europe

The final chapter of this book highlights three very special places in the Appalachian Mountains of West Virginia. The history of these three unique locations is intriguing yet few people can relate what happened in these places many years ago. I have gathered much of the known information about these locations and assembled a fairly comprehensive rendition of each locale's history. What follows is a detailed description of the events that make these three places very special and interesting. Parts of this chapter have been published previously in the *Wonderful West Virginia* magazine.

The Hudson River Valley in New York State has its well-known legend of Sleepy Hollow and, not to be outdone, Braxton County, West Virginia's Elk River also has its legend – the legend of Strange Creek. Both legends have their roots in true local history. Both legends are shaded with the color of folklore. The legend surrounding Strange Creek is swirled in mystery, coated with truth, and embellished by local tales. Whether the legend of Strange Creek is mostly true or just a good story passed down through the years, one thing is certain. It has become a piece of the region's folklore and part of the West Virginia's oral tradition through its constant telling and re-telling throughout the years.

How did Strange Creek get such a – well- strange name? Strange Creek began as Turkey Run – a stream originating on the western side of Powell's Mountain in Nicholas County and flowing through Clay County to end in Braxton County. There it enters the Elk River near the village of Strange Creek. The creek itself is charming and a wader's delight, but those attributes alone do not make this stream special. The same could be said about any one of the other countless creeks and streams that meander through scenic West Virginia. Long ago an event occurred on the banks of this stream that gave birth to the legend of Strange Creek. This event changed the name of Turkey Run to Strange Creek forever and caused this meandering brook to become famous throughout the neighboring counties.

The story begins with the first white settlers who moved into the region. Early in the history of Braxton County settlement, when Native Americans were the only inhabitants of the region, John Allison contracted to have his 11,000 acres of land surveyed. This was the first land survey ever conducted in Braxton County and was done in 1784. Only a few years later, in 1789 or 1790, Benjamin Carpenter and his family became the first permanent white settlers to move into the area. The Carpenters built log cabins and started a small settlement near Centralia along the Holly River. Moving one's family to this area was risky business at the time. White settlers in western Virginia (as this area was called then) had been subjected to regular and ferocious attacks from the Indians in the area since the 1770's or earlier. Apparently, the lure of building their own home in this wild and beautiful country was stronger than the fear of Indian attacks. The Carpenter family cut down trees and built cabins to start a new life on their newly acquired holdings.

Sadly, within five years of their settlement, the lives of the Carpenter family were tragically altered. Popular history records the tale that Benjamin Carpenter and his wife were murdered in 1792 by two Indians who discovered the white settlers" presence by noticing wood chips floating in the Holly River. The wood chips alerted the Indians to the fact that white settlers were in the vicinity because only white folks used axes for wood chopping. It was not a difficult task for the Indians to travel upstream and find and murder the Carpenters.

Even though violence such as this was a regular occurrence in the region, surveyors continued to survey large land grants in present-day central West Virginia. Samuel Young was anxious to have his sizeable land grant along the beautiful Elk and Holly Rivers surveyed in spite of the simmering violence. Although dates vary slightly, around the year 1795 a surveying party led by Henry Jackson entered this scenic region to survey Young's land grant.

One of the surveying party, a young surveyor named William Strange, ventured with the group into the wild timbered country near the Elk River. There is some disagreement as to Strange's role in the party and the role he played varies widely depending on what account of this story you choose to believe. Because of his youth and unfamiliarity with the wilderness country of the Holly and Elk Rivers, it was highly unlikely that he was the guide or advance scout for the surveying party. Charles Dodrill in *Heritage of a Pioneer* assigns the role of party guide to Jerry Carpenter, Benjamin's brother. Benjamin lived near Sutton Lake and was a skilled and ingenious woodsman.

Some accounts claim Strange was the hunter of the group and kept the camp cook supplied with fresh meat. However, Peter Silitch writes in the *West Virginia Encyclopedia* that Strange was more likely the group's cook since he was so young and inexperienced. He probably had been recruited as camp cook by the surveying party when they were encamped near Beverly in Randolph

County. As the cook, he was certainly given charge of the packhorses.

Regardless of William Strange's role in the surveying party, he became separated from the rest of his party and found himself hopelessly lost on the Elk River not far from the mouth of the Holly River. One story states that he got lost when trying to take some pack horses to meet up with the surveyors who had gone on ahead of the main party. The night after the rendezvous, Dodrill, in *Heritage of the Pioneer*, claims Strange was instructed to follow the Holly River to its confluence with the Elk River. He was then told to follow the Elk until he came to the Carpenter settlement where the party would meet up with him the second night.

The story goes that Strange came to a fork in the path on Holly River a mile from its mouth. He took the wrong path and, instead of fording the Holly and finding its junction with the Elk, soon became hopelessly lost. The path that he took crossed the mountain and finally arrived at the banks of the Elk. Several accounts claim Strange panicked and began to walk up the Elk River along the shore. Unable to find its meeting place with the Holly and encountering impassible falls and narrows, Strange became confused and back-tracked to his starting place. Evidence indicated he tied his horse to a nearby bush. Skip Johnson, author of *River on the Rocks*, claims that anyone who has deer hunted in the area around the Elk and Cranberry Rivers can understand the confusion with the rivers that must have afflicted Strange. No one knows for sure how the story ends at this point. One thing, however, is certain. William Strange was never seen or heard of again.

The surveying groups searched the banks of the rivers and surrounding forest the next day. Jerry Carpenter, the group's guide, led the party on a diligent hunt for the young cook. One member of the group fired off a shot in hopes of alerting Strange that help was near. Carpenter chastised him, however, out of fear that the gunshot would alert the hostile Indians in the area. The search was finally called-off because Strange had completely vanished. No sign of him was ever found by the party and the mystery of his disappearance simmered for several years.

Several years later, a mysterious discovery was made by local hunters searching for wild game. These hunters supposedly located Strange's remains on Strange Creek (still called Turkey Run at the time). Some accounts of the legend claim that Strange's gun, and not his remains, was found on the banks of the creek. We may never know for sure what evidence was actually located to prove the young cook perished near the creek.

It is at this point that young William Strange becomes immortalized in legend and story. Along with his bleached and weathered bones, legend has it that Strange left his legacy in the form of a carving on the base of a beech tree (or sycamore, depending on which version you believe) near the mouth of Strange Creek. Dodrill writes the inscription was found by hunters and read "Strange is my name and I am on strange ground and strange it is that I cannot be found." Another account of the carving recited by Dille residents was "My name is Strange, and I'm on strange ground, I'm lost in the woods and I know I'll not be found." Regardless of the wording of the rhyme, it is very clear that Strange may have realized his party would never discover him. He was probably confused, hungry, disoriented and very lost and running out of hope that he would ever be found. Carving his own epitaph into the tree could have been his way of making a mark for his rescuers to find in this beautiful, but hostile wilderness. Some folks question the existence of his carved epitaph. The beech tree has long since vanished. Even the exact location of Strange's demise is one of much debate. Accounts vary, but the one most often told is that he died near where Big Run comes into Strange Creek about two miles below

Dille. Whether one believes this legend or not, one fact is certain. Turkey Run became Strange Creek due to this young man's misfortune and wrong choice of path.

Home Guards and Booger Hole:
Rough Beginnings of a Nice Community

Booger Hole, a small rural community in Clay County, West Virginia, is located not far off St. Rt. 16 and close to the Big Otter Exit on I-79. Today, Booger Hole is peaceful and prosperous in a quiet and unassuming way. Driving past the comfortable homes and picturesque farms, one would never guess at its well-hidden past full of murders, mayhem, and violence. Residents of Booger Hole are long-removed from the distant memories of lurid crimes and the tainted past of their hollow. While the past is but a distant memory in Booger Hole residents' daily life today, events begun during the Civil War forever changed the course of their town's history.

For most folks, the Civil War stirs up memories of hard-fought battles such as Bull Run and Gettysburg. It saddens our hearts to remember how the war divided families, took countless lives in their prime, and brought enormous grief to our nation. Our history books are full of stories about the valor and battle victories of such legendary generals as Stonewall Jackson and Robert E. Lee and most of us think of these brave men when West Virginia's Civil War past is mentioned. But a few of us remember tales of other brave folks in the mountain state. We think about ordinary West Virginians who tried to lead normal lives while the events of a war they scarcely understood swirled around them. One group of ordinary citizens who played a little-known role during the Civil War in West Virginia served their cause by joining the local militias. These local militias were called Home Guard units.

During the spring of 1861, after Virginia adopted an ordinance to secede from the Union, Union leadership immediately began to recruit the men of western Virginia into Federal service. On May 14, 1862 Congress passed an act authorizing the citizens of each county to form Home Guard units to act as policing authorities during the War. Those individuals who wanted to serve their country but were too old, too young, or too sickly to enlist in the army were therefore given the opportunity to join the Home Guard in their own county. Each Home Guard was only allowed to serve in their own county and was not paid any salary or wages. In addition, each man had to provide his own weapons and ammunition and received food rations only when serving his allotted 30 days of active duty.

Although they were not entitled to Federal pensions or West Virginia Civil War medals, members of the Home Guard served a valuable role by guarding the railroads, bridges, and other important structures in what is now the state of West Virginia. The Home Guard also scouted the area for the enlisted troops and chased Confederate supporters whose raids and robberies were a continual plague to the northern counties. Boyd B. Stutler, in his book *West Virginia in the Civil War*, states that the central counties of West Virginia during the spring of 1861, were infested with gangs of confederate sympathizers who terrorized the citizens by looting, pillaging, stealing horses, and burning barns. These raiders spread grief and alarm throughout counties of Calhoun, Clay, Braxton, and Gilmer by stealing the scanty food supplies that families had managed to put up for the coming winter.

The Home Guards were organized by both sides of the conflict to protect the families and property of those fighting in the war. However, all too often these local militias did just the opposite – they used their authority to steal, confiscate, and even destroy the property of other folks. Minnora Proudfoot's reminiscences of her childhood during the Civil War in *Pioneer Home Life and Civil War Hardships* tell us that both the Home Guards and the deserters were labeled as bushwhackers during this time period because they went "whacking" around destroying and stealing everything that wasn't nailed down.

Renegade groups were valued by the Confederate forces because they created a distraction for Union troops and kept many men at home defending their farms instead of fighting for the Union. An interesting offshoot of this partisan violence was the opportunity to wreak a little home-grown revenge on one's neighbors. The Civil War created an opportunity for folks to take back property they deemed theirs or exact a payback for suffered wrongs. Unfortunately, many times these roaming bands of marauders committed heinous crimes of murder, arson, and robbery while acting out of personal vendettas. Political causes only served as a façade or excuse for the real motive – revenge or sheer criminal activity.

One of the most active and feared of the various groups roaming the central counties of West Virginia was the Moccasin Rangers. The Moccasin Rangers operated under the leadership of at least a half dozen self-styled leaders and was based in Calhoun County. One such leader stands out as particularly aggressive and larger-than-life – Perry Conley. Perry Conley, sometimes called the "Quantrel of West Virginia," came from Calhoun County as did most of his followers. He was reputed to be a large strapping man who could ride horseback up to 60 miles a day and whip any man who challenged him to fight. His feats of strength and audacity were legendary and local residents lived in fear of his group.

Perry Conley's Moccasin Rangers included Conley's girlfriend, Nancy Hart, who later earned the title of the "lady guerrilla" of the Rangers. Nancy met Conley shortly after her brother-in-law, William Price of Roane County, was murdered by a band of Union Home Guards.

Nancy's vicious temper and shooting prowess earned her a reputation as good as any man's that rode with the Rangers. She not only successfully spied on Union troops, but endearing herself with smiles and sugary language, also killed several of them for their trouble. After the demise of her boyfriend, Perry Conley, in 1862, Nancy continued her service to the Confederacy by serving as a guide for General Stonewall Jackson. Hart's grave can be found at Manning's Knob near the Nicholas-Greenbrier county line although some dispute that her body is actually buried there.

One of those unfortunate enough to make the acquaintance of one of these renegade groups, possibly the Moccasin Rangers, was James Rogers, a hard-working man of excellent reputation in his community of Booger Hole. Rogers was instrumental in founding a Home Guard unit in Booger Hole to protect the interests of families on both sides of the conflict. The West Virginia Militia Database names this Home Guard unit the Clay County 126th Militia which was later reorganized into the Clay County Scouts. According to the 1860 Federal census records of Clay County, Rogers was 47 years of age in 1861 and had taken the Home Guard oath on September 28, 1861.

One frosty October night in 1862, Rogers and a friend, Solomon Carpenter (some records call him Jesse) were on patrol in Booger Hole. They were looking for renegades who might be passing through the area with evil intent. They came across a group, possibly Conley's Moccasin Rangers, and followed them. Identifying some of the group as Confederate sympathizers who lived in the local community, Rogers and Carpenter did not pursue or engage them but instead, went to their own homes for the night. Unfortunately, the mercy Rogers and Carpenter showed the Moccasin Rangers was not reciprocated. Later that same night, Conley and his Rangers rousted Rogers and Carpenter from their warm beds. They dragged the two men up the hollow and tied them to a tree. After shooting Rogers and Carpenter repeatedly, the Rangers left their dead bodies to be found by family members the next morning.

Even local Confederate sympathizers were horrified and sickened by the senseless brutality of Conley and his followers in the murders of Rogers and Carpenter. Both sides of the conflict chased Conley's group until Perry Conley was finally ambushed by Union troops in 1862 near Webster Springs. They mortally wounded him so he was unable to escape yet he fought like a cornered animal until they ended up clubbing him to death with their rifle butts. Despised equally by both sides, Conley may have realized it could just as easily have been Confederate guns that ended his life.

When the Civil War was over, the Moccasin Rangers and other Home Guard groups disbanded and returned to their homes. In Booger Hole, left-over violence and anarchy persisted as bushwhackers confiscated the property of others and terrorized neighbors. Peace was not to appear in Booger Hole for many years following the official end of the war. Home Guard from both sides, returning to their homes in the area, confiscated property of those not fortunate enough to survive the conflict and the crime wave continued. The rough and lawless way of life many had learned during the Civil War was not easily forgotten. It soon seemed that the devil himself had come home to roost in Booger Hole.

Violence began during the Civil War seemed to breed and propagate without end in Booger Hole. Quarrels and disagreements that might have died a natural death anywhere else intensified in Booger Hole after the Civil War. Mary Lucinda Curry's well-known book, *Booger Hole: Mysteries, Ghost Tales, and Strange Occurrences,* documents Booger Hole's lurid history with tales of murder, crime, and people disappearing never to be seen again. Horse thieves, murderers, highwaymen, and other criminals hid out from the law in Booger Hole and even brave lawmen were hesitant to enter the hollow day or night.

It was during this lawless and frightening time that Booger Hole got its distinctive name. Before the Civil War, the area was simply called Richardson's Run of Rush Fork Hollow according to Curry. Once Booger Hole became the hideout of the lawless and criminal element, Curry writes that you could ride through Booger Hole at night by the flash of gun fire in greeting.

Bob Weaver, in his article entitled "Hurrah for Booger Hole," tells of strange disappearances, of people who entered Booger Hole never to be seen again. More than one peddler disappeared in Booger Holler and an old woman, Lacey O'Brien Boggs, was shot through the window of her house as she sat peeling apples. The story goes that Mrs. Boggs knew too much about the death of a pack peddler. She was heard telling others that she knew where he was buried. A father and son were charged with the murder but they were never brought to justice. They claimed the old woman was a witch and had cast a spell on them. Lacking sufficient evidence, they were released.

Another Booger Hole citizen also met an untimely end. Preston Tanner made the unfortunate decision to play cards one night with a young man named Howard Sampson. Apparently Tanner won once too often and died of a crushed skull. Howard Sampson and his father, Andrew, were accused of murdering Tanner with a claw hammer and then burning his house to the ground to cover the crime. The neighbors in Booger Hole knew young Sampson had a motive for the murder and it wasn't just anger over losing at cards. The young man had often been heard proclaiming his love for Tanner's beautiful wife. He made no secret of his desire to have her even if it meant murdering her husband, Preston. The fine folks of Booger

Hole also knew Sampson had a rowdy nature. He often started fights and regularly shot-up the neighborhood so they knew he was capable of anything.

Tanner's death inflamed Booger Hole citizens and they formed a lynch mob. The mob rode to the Clay County courthouse and demanded young Howard Sampson be turned over to them for hanging. Only the eloquent pleadings of a local attorney spared Sampson from the angry mob. Howard Sampson was convicted of the murder of Preston Tanner and sentenced to life in prison while his father was released to return to his home in Booger Hole. The angry group from Booger Hole were not satisfied that justice had been served, however, and they determined that the murdering, thieving, and criminal escapades that had so long made Booger Hole a place ruled by fear, would have to stop.

The citizens of Booger Hole issued a handbill that proclaimed the organization of the Clay County Mob. They posted this handbill over the entire county and declared that they aimed to run every scoundrel and murderer out of the county or kill them. They named names and promised to catch and hang every thief, murderer, and arsonist in the area if they did not leave the state of West Virginia. The Clay County Mob enacted their own form of vigilante justice by dynamiting and burning down the shanties of those identified as criminals in Booger Hole. Trouble-makers and lawbreakers did not lose any time fleeing Booger Hole. Apparently taking the law into their own hands solved the problem because Booger Hole became a safe place to raise one's family once again.

Today, Booger Hole is a sleepy hamlet with modern houses and farms – a far cry from "The Hole" of infamous myth and legend. Stories of the unsolved crimes committed in Booger Hole are still told around the table by locals in Booger Hole – a testament to the rough beginnings of a nice community.

The Ritchie Mines

If one is brave enough to venture into the rugged forested hills and ravines of the Richie Mines Wildlife Management area (WMA), one may stumble upon a hollow that is deeper and darker than most. The temperature here is several degrees cooler than the surrounding area. Close your eyes and imagine you hear a faint train whistle carried on winds that have suddenly turned chilly. Welcome! You have just stumbled upon the few remains of what was once a thriving boomtown of 2,500 people along Macfarlan Creek. What prompted the growth of this boomtown and where has it gone? Why are the mines said to be haunted? Just what happened here in this remote and little-known part of Ritchie County?

Lost in time and almost forgotten, the Ritchie Mines in Macfarlan, Ritchie County, harbor ghosts who could tell tales of enormous wealth and fortunes lost. This was the site of a mining boomtown, a prosperous asphalt mine, and a railroad. Now only the overgrown railroad bed and the remains of an old smelting furnace made of handmade red clay bricks remain of that boomtown. Those who recall the time when the mines were operating are few in number these days but legends and stories are still told about this once thriving boomtown on cold winter nights.

The Ritchie Mines are rare natural asphalt mines located north of the tiny village of Macfarlan. Robert Lawrence Cokeley, writing in the *Oil Man's Magazine* in 1910, called the Ritchie Mines one of the wonders of the world. Although there are other asphalt mines in Texas, Utah, Oklahoma, California, Trinidad, and Venezuela, the asphalt taken from the Ritchie Mines was unique in formation and chemical analysis and stood in a class by itself. Only one other mine even remotely compared in asphalt composition and formation. This mine was located in Nova Scotia and was depleted long before the Ritchie Mines began operations.

The story of the Ritchie Mines begins with a geological freak of nature that occurred long ago during prehistoric times. An anticline, or arched upheaval of solid rock, occurred when the Appalachian Mountains were uplifted. Then, instead of the far more common vertical displacement of most faults, the ground moved apart horizontally and a five-foot fissure, or crack in the rock layers, opened. Oil and gas seeped into the fissure and formed a gummy substance as it oxidized through exposure to air. The substance eventually hardened into a coal-like material. This process took hundreds of thousands of years, transforming enormous quantities of oil into this rare and precious natural asphalt material called grahamite after J.A. and J.L. Graham.

How was this deposit of precious asphalt discovered? The answer dates back to 1852 – a time during which West Virginia was still the western corner of Virginia. A farmer, Frederick Lemon, was tending his cattle along Macfarlan Creek after a long rainy season. Massive flooding exposed an outcropping of shiny material that Lemon reasoned must be coal. Camouflaging his find with brush and leaves, he hurried off to purchase the land. James Ankrom says it took six years of negotiating before Lemon was able to buy the land. In the meantime, other folks found the "coal" and began to burn it in their stoves. Unfortunately, this "coal" exploded and nearly burned houses and forges down so people gave up trying to use it as fuel. Lemon also tried to burn this "coal" and was disgusted at the way it melted and ran like tar. He sold the land in 1859, one year after buying it from John Webb and Robert Marshall, to Nelson Beall (some sources refer to him as "Bell") of Maryland. Conflicting sources differ at the price Beall (Bell) paid Lemon for the land. Robert L. Cokeley, writing for the *Oil Man's Magazine*, states Lemon received the tidy sum of $75,000 but James Ankrom quotes the selling price of $7,000. At any rate, Lemon was reportedly glad to be rid of it!

Beall mined the "coal" and transported it by mule train to a location where enormous retorts converted it into oil. The *Oil Man's Magazine* claimed that one ton of this "coal" produced 140 to 165 gallons of oil. Robert Cokeley claimed that this asphalt sold for $90 per ton during these pre-Civil War days.

People flocked into the Ritchie Mines and a boom town blossomed on Macfarlan Creek. Minnie Kendall Lowther, in her book, *History of Ritchie County* informs us that a "large number of Irish people" settled their families here at this time. The population of this mining town grew rapidly as the mines continued to produce this rare asphalt. Men left their farms and bought land up and down Macfarlan Creek in the hope that they would "strike it rich!" A large brick hotel was built and a village with paved streets marked the site of this boomtown. A boulevard was built along Macfarlan Creek and the creek itself was re-routed and channeled by a wall of cut stone. The mine owners cleared a yearly profit of one million dollars and people kept pouring into the area to make their fortunes. Beall finally sold his holdings to the Ritchie Coal Oil Company for three million dollars.

The asphalt lode had to be mined by pick and shovel in an unusual manner because of the vertical nature of the seam (usually coal was found in horizontal layers). Approximately 100 miners started digging at the top of the hill and drifted back into the hillside working at a vertical height of around six feet. Once they depleted the seam they were working, they started mining another seam below it. In this way, the miners kept mining further and further downward towards the bed of Macfarlan Creek. Mining was very dangerous in those days. The walls of the mine were not shored up and loose rock continually fell down on the miners as they worked.

The Ritchie Mines had three openings and two tipples. The chief opening of the mine was situated on a branch of Macfarlan Creek where the stream had eroded into the asphalt deposit. The miners worked from both sides of the stream to mine the asphalt and haul the coal to a common tipple. The third mine opening was located on the other side of the hill where the valley of Macfarlan Creek bisected the asphalt deposit. The Calico Railroad tracks ran around the base of this steep hill with the vertical seam of asphalt towering overhead. A chute carried the ore down the steep hillside and into waiting cars standing on the railroad track. Hard-working mules were soon replaced with a little engine called the Ritchie, commissioned to pull the heavy cars loaded with asphalt ore.

The Civil War interrupted the mining here in Macfarlan Creek. Miners quit and the threat that roaming bands of marauders would torch the mines was always in the back of everyone's mind. No new veins of ore were discovered and the price of oil ranged from $20 per barrel to zero. The owners of the Ritchie Coal Oil Company steadily lost money and the speculators who had purchased pricey acreage on Macfarlan Creek now despaired of selling their land at all. Most of them were ruined and lost everything as prices plummeted. Some committed suicide and others were committed to asylums. The fortunes that had been made virtually overnight disappeared just as swiftly after the darkness of the war years.

In the meantime, a new use had been discovered for this strange form of coal – street paving. Pennsylvania Avenue became the one of the first paved roads in the nation and it was paved with asphalt from the Ritchie Mines. When the King of Prussia in Germany heard about the famous material mined in the Ritchie Mines, he soon became one of the Mines' best customers, importing several hundred tons of asphalt across the ocean to pave the streets of Germany's capital. Soon streets in London and the Hague were being paved by asphalt from the Ritchie Mines, too!

However, problems began to confront the Ritchie Coal Oil Company on two fronts. First, asphalt deposits were being discovered in other locations around the world, and the Ritchie Mines no longer had international markets for their product. Oil was also being discovered in abundance so it was no longer profitable to convert the asphalt into oil. Secondly, the Ritchie Mines were becoming more and more difficult to work. Pumps operated night and day to keep the heavy and constant flows of water out of the fissure. The miners were afraid they were about to tap into a huge underground lake and many refused to continue digging. By then, the deepest part of the one and one-half mile long fissure was being mined at a depth of three hundred feet below Macfarlan Creek. The asphalt was reported as being very soft and the men were terrified of crashing through into a lake of oil. One report claims a miner sunk to his knees in the soft asphalt and was rescued with great difficulty.

Even with excellent ventilation, mine gases continued to build-up and threaten the welfare and safety of those working in the mines. The danger in mining this substance occurred because oil and gas would come into the vein so rapidly during the mining process that the miners could not remove it quickly enough. Explosions occurred easily when a miner's carbide light would cause a pocket of gas to explode. James Ankrom states that two explosions occurred in 1873 when fine dry dust ignited from the miners' lamps. Several men died from the explosions. One night in 1873, after the men had quit working, the gas exploded, killing the night watchman and the mules and destroying the stables inside the mines. In addition to these tragedies, the asphalt vein disappeared due to a rock barrier in the vein. Engineers failed to relocate the vein and many miners were laid off and sought other employment. Soon after the layoffs, a third and far more devastating explosion took place collapsing a main tunnel. Rescue workers tried but failed to rescue or recover the 30 miners bodies leaving them entombed forever in the mines. The remaining miners (many of them superstitious) refused to report back to work because the mines were said to be haunted by those killed in the explosion. Since the company was barely clearing a profit, the decision was made to abandon the mine and sell the railroad engine.

The once-booming mining town started to empty out as families gradually drifted away to pursue other livelihoods. Some moved to nearby towns of Oxbow and Silver Run. Ritchie Gazette reporter Janet Hodge wrote, "…what it took 20 years to build, only took a matter of months to take on the appearance of a ghost town." As people cleared out, the dark hollow was said to be haunted by the spirits of those killed in the explosion. Few residents remained in this once-thriving mining town. The two boarding houses, the blacksmith's shop, and the sawmill rapidly closed as people moved. The mines, as well as the railroad and boomtown, fell into a dilapidated state of ruins and neglect. Then, in 1885, H.S. Wilson of Parkersburg purchased the land, mines, and railroad. He renamed the little Calico Railroad the Cairo and Kanawha Valley (C&KV) Railroad, building new tracks over the old Calico Railroad right-of-way. He extended the railroad to Mellin in 1892 and finally to the river at Macfarlan in 1894. Wilson employed a few men to work the Ritchie Mines but the output was negligible. Then, the richest salt sand field ever discovered in oil history was found in Cairo. The C& KV transported oil and the Ritchie Mines once again was forgotten. The remains of the once-famous boomtown were overtaken by weeds and wild animals were the only living inhabitants.

In 1904, the Ritchie Coal Mines Co. purchased the Ritchie Mines and began operation. The operation was horribly inefficient. The mine fissure had filled in almost completely with eroded soil and debris from the nearby hillsides and mining was a tediously slow and difficult process. Primitive mining operations continued until 1910 with coal being dug and loaded into coffee sacks and transported to the surface by a small engine outside the crevice. Sometimes the asphalt was loaded into barrels and hauled up to the surface, emptied, and lowered again. The mining gradually ceased and the mines closed completely. Over the next 70 years, the Ritchie Mines once again fell into a state of neglect and disrepair. Weeds grew up and covered the railroad right-of-way. The few buildings left standing eventually collapsed and their roofs caved-in.

In 1983, two young men, David Westfall of Smithville and Mark Gaston of Mellin, fulfilled their boyhood dreams to explore the Ritchie Mines. Well-equipped with headlamps and climbing gear, they rappelled 100 feet down into the crevice of the Ritchie Mines to explore the dark underground cavity. They found things much the same as they were the day the last miner left in 1910 – picks stuck in the dirt, shovels laying on the mine floor. Janet Hodge, reporter for the Ritchie Gazette, reported that less than a year after these two young men explored the depths of the Ritchie Mines, a cave-in occurred which blocked off the mine entrance they had used.

Today the land surrounding the Ritchie Mines has largely reverted back to wilderness. In 1989, the West Virginia Department of Natural Resources purchased the Ritchie Mines as part of a 1,731- acre tract for a price of over $300,000. This site is now part of the 2,300 acre Ritchie Mines Wildlife Management area (WMA) and is still very rugged and steep terrain. The old Ritchie Mine still exists – a 30' to 50' deep, 36 inch wide mining trench running from the top of one hill down into the hollow and back up the side of another hill. Tall Timber, Inc. has timbered the area and its logging roads bisect the older oil and gas road cuts making navigation a cumbersome and difficult process at best. The area is accessible only by four-wheel drive vehicles and on foot. Caution should be taken around the mines as there are numerous holes and shafts covered by leaves and debris. The Ritchie Mines area can be safely hunted for deer turkey, squirrel, grouse and raccoon if one observes precautions around the site of the mine; however, camping is not permitted.

Not long after the DNR bought the Ritchie Mines, there was substantial interest in having it registered on the National Register of Historic Places to preserve its historical significance and generate tourism to the area. However, since then lack of funding and other obstacles have put these plans on hold indefinitely.

On a sunny day, the cool, dark hollow containing the old ghost town's remains does not seem too scary. The sight movement of brush caught by the corner of your eye is only a deer vanishing from sight or a rabbit scurrying for cover. But as shadows lengthen and fall, one's thoughts are drawn back to the bustling town that once existed there and the miners still entombed in the old mine shafts. A distant train whistle blows and the faint smell of oily rock drifts in on the breeze....

Epilogue

"In some manner, a mountain country places its mark on those who dwell within its shadows. Scots carry with them a Highland pride of birth and pace, even though they may wander thousands of miles from heather-covered moors. Natives of Switzerland see the Alps, although these peaks are far below the horizon. And thus it is with those nurtured in Appalachia – they leave, but they look back, remembering those pleasant things. The land has claimed them and its ties will not be severed."

Maurice Brooks, from
The Appalachians, 1965